The Holocaust

GREAT DISASTERS
REFORMS and RAMIFICATIONS

The Holocaust

Judy L. Hasday, Ed.M.

CHELSEA HOUSE PUBLISHERS
Philadelphia

Special thanks to Sara Paul for sharing her story with me. In times of difficulty, I will draw strength from your heartening words, "From the ashes, look what I have."

Frontispiece: Survivors of Ebensee, a satellite camp of the notorious Mauthausen concentration camp, photographed May 7, 1945, the day after Allied troops liberated them.

CHELSEA HOUSE PUBLISHERS

Editor in Chief Sally Cheney
Associate Editor in Chief Kim Shinners
Production Manager Pamela Loos
Art Director Sara Davis

Staff for THE HOLOCAUST

Senior Editor John Ziff
Picture Researcher Judy L. Hasday
Cover Designer Takeshi Takahashi
Layout 21st Century Publishing and Communications, Inc.

First Printing

1 3 5 7 9 8 6 4 2

The Chelsea House World Wide Web address is
http://www.chelseahouse.com

Library of Congress Cataloging-in-Publication Data

Hasday, Judy L. 1957–
The Holocaust / by Judy L. Hasday.
    p. cm. — (Great disasters)
Includes bibliographical references (p.   ) and index.

ISBN 0-7910-5790-9 (alk. paper)

1. Holocaust, Jewish (1939–1945)—Juvenile literature.
2. Antisemitism—Germany—History—20th century—
Juvenile literature. 3. Germany—Ethnic relations—Juvenile
literature. [1. Holocaust, Jewish (1939–1945)] I. Title. II. Series.

D804.34.H37 2001
940.53'18—dc21

2001028522

Contents

GREAT DISASTERS
REFORMS and RAMIFICATIONS

THE *APOLLO 1* AND
CHALLENGER DISASTERS

BHOPAL

THE BLACK DEATH

THE BLIZZARD OF 1888

THE BOMBING OF HIROSHIMA

THE CHERNOBYL NUCLEAR DISASTER

THE DUST BOWL

THE EXPLOSION OF TWA FLIGHT 800

THE *EXXON VALDEZ*

THE GALVESTON HURRICANE

THE GREAT CHICAGO FIRE

THE GREAT PLAGUE AND
FIRE OF LONDON

THE *HINDENBURG*

THE HOLOCAUST

THE INFLUENZA PANDEMIC OF 1918

THE IRISH POTATO FAMINE

THE JOHNSTOWN FLOOD

LOVE CANAL

THE MUNICH OLYMPICS

NUCLEAR SUBMARINE DISASTERS

THE OKLAHOMA CITY BOMBING

PEARL HARBOR

THE SALEM WITCH TRIALS

THE SAN FRANCISCO EARTHQUAKE
OF 1906

THE SPANISH INQUISITION

THE STOCK MARKET CRASH OF 1929

TERRORISM

THREE MILE ISLAND

THE *TITANIC*

THE TRIANGLE SHIRTWAIST COMPANY
FIRE OF 1911

THE WACO SIEGE

THE WORLD TRADE CENTER BOMBING

Jill McCaffrey
National Chairman
Armed Forces Emergency Services
American Red Cross

Introduction

Disasters have always been a source of fascination and awe. Tales of a great flood that nearly wipes out all life are among humanity's oldest recorded stories, dating at least from the second millennium B.C., and they appear in cultures from the Middle East to the Arctic Circle to the southernmost tip of South America and the islands of Polynesia. Typically gods are at the center of these ancient disaster tales—which is perhaps not too surprising, given the fact that the tales originated during a time when human beings were at the mercy of natural forces they did not understand.

To a great extent, we still are at the mercy of nature, as anyone who reads the newspapers or watches nightly news broadcasts can attest.

Hurricanes, earthquakes, tornados, wildfires, and floods continue to exact a heavy toll in suffering and death, despite our considerable knowledge of the workings of the physical world. If science has offered only limited protection from the consequences of natural disasters, it has in no way diminished our fascination with them. Perhaps that's because the scale and power of natural disasters force us as individuals to confront our relatively insignificant place in the physical world and remind us of the fragility and transience of our lives. Perhaps it's because we can imagine ourselves in the midst of dire circumstances and wonder how we would respond. Perhaps it's because disasters seem to bring out the best and worst instincts of humanity: altruism and selfishness, courage and cowardice, generosity and greed.

As one of the national chairmen of the American Red Cross, a humanitarian organization that provides relief for victims of disasters, I have had the privilege of seeing some of humanity's best instincts. I have witnessed communities pulling together in the face of trauma; I have seen thousands of people answer the call to help total strangers in their time of need.

Of course, helping victims after a tragedy is not the only way, or even the best way, to deal with disaster. In many cases planning and preparation can minimize damage and loss of life—or even avoid a disaster entirely. For, as history repeatedly shows, many disasters are caused not by nature but by human folly, shortsightedness, and unethical conduct. For example, when a land developer wanted to create a lake for his exclusive resort club in Pennsylvania's Allegheny Mountains in 1880, he ignored expert warnings and cut corners in reconstructing an earthen dam. On May 31, 1889, the dam gave way, unleashing 20 million tons of water on the towns below. The Johnstown Flood, the deadliest in American history, claimed more than 2,200 lives. Greed and negligence would figure prominently in the Triangle Shirtwaist Company fire in 1911. Deplorable conditions in the garment sweatshop, along with a failure to give any thought to the safety of workers, led to the tragic deaths of 146 persons. Technology outstripped wisdom only a year later, when the designers of the luxury liner *Titanic* smugly declared their state-of-the-art ship "unsinkable," seeing no need to provide lifeboat capacity for everyone onboard. On the night of April 14, 1912, more than 1,500 passengers and crew paid for this hubris with their lives after the ship collided with an iceberg and sank. But human catastrophes aren't always the unforeseen consequences of carelessness or folly. In the 1940s the leaders of Nazi Germany purposefully and systematically set out to exterminate all Jews, along with Gypsies, homosexuals, the mentally ill, and other so-called undesirables. More recently terrorists have targeted random members of society, blowing up airplanes and buildings in an effort to advance their political agendas.

The books in the GREAT DISASTERS: REFORMS AND RAMIFICATIONS series examine these and other famous disasters, natural and human made. They explain the causes of the disasters, describe in detail how events unfolded, and paint vivid portraits of the people caught up in dangerous circumstances. But these books are more than just accounts of what happened to whom and why. For they place the disasters in historical perspective, showing how people's attitudes and actions changed and detailing the steps society took in the wake of each calamity. And in the end, the most important lesson we can learn from any disaster—as well as the most fitting tribute to those who suffered and died—is how to avoid a repeat in the future.

A History of Hatred

"[Jews] have sincerely tried everywhere to merge with the national communities in which we live, seeking only to preserve the faith of our fathers. It is not permitted us. In vain are we loyal patriots . . . in vain do we make the same sacrifices of life and property as our fellow citizens; in vain do we strive to enhance the fame of our native lands in the arts and sciences, or her wealth by trade and commerce. In our native lands where we have lived for centuries we are still decried as aliens."

—journalist Theodor Herzl, advocate of a Jewish homeland in Palestine

January 30, 1933, marked the beginning of one of the darkest periods in 20th-century history. That day, Adolf Hitler became chancellor (prime minister) of Germany. From his new position, Hitler almost immediately began taking steps to fulfill the twisted vision he had held for years: the creation of a "pure," master German race.

Hitler's deep-rooted hatred of Jews and other "unde-sirables"—including Gypsies, Jehovah's Witnesses, homosexuals, and Communists—fueled his resolve to "cleanse" his native country of those who he believed contaminated German life and culture. Between 1933 and 1945, people who fell into these categories were sub-jected to increasingly harsh treatment. Ultimately, in one of the worst tragedies in recorded history, millions of these "undesirables" were methodically exterminated.

Hitler believed that all peoples were inferior to Aryans, a supposed race having typically Nordic features, including fair skin, blond hair, and blue eyes. In reality, anthropologists—scientists who study the physical and social characteristics of humans—don't even recognize the existence of such a race.

If Aryans were at the top of the Nazis' confused racial pyramid, Jews were at the very bottom. Indeed, Hitler reserved his most passionate hatred for Jews, whom he saw as a "parasitic, enemy race." (Once again, however, any competent anthropologist would point out that being Jew-ish has nothing to do with race.) With his henchmen, including Hermann Göring, Heinrich Himmler, Reinhard Heydrich, and Adolf Eichmann, Hitler devised a "Final Solution" to what he termed "the Jewish problem." In short, the Nazis formulated a plan to exterminate every Jew in Europe. The horror is that Hitler nearly succeeded: in less than a decade, two-thirds of the Jewish population of Europe—more than six million Jewish men, women, and children—were annihilated.

Today, that methodical extermination is referred to as the Holocaust, a word that originally referred to a raging fire causing total destruction. Because of the way Hitler's victims were killed, and because of the vast scope and the speed with which they were eliminated, the term is now commonly applied to the mass killings perpetrated by Germany under Nazism. In more recent years, the word *genocide*—defined as "the planned killing of an entire cultural or racial group of people"—has been used to describe the slaughter of Jews and other groups in Europe during World War II.

The type of hatred behind Hitler's crusade was not new. For much of the two millennia in which Jews lived in Europe, they faced continual discrimination and persecution. Even Hitler's anti-Semitic (anti-Jewish) rhetoric derived from centuries of hate and distrust.

The history of the Jews is a saga of exile. For thousands of years Jews struggled to coexist with—and often, simply to survive among—other peoples in foreign lands. Always the dream was to return to what they believed was their homeland.

Jewish history begins with the Old Testament biblical figure of Abraham, a Hebrew who lived around 2300 B.C. Born in Mesopotamia, Abraham moved to Canaan (present day Israel), where God promised him numerous heirs and pledged Canaan to him for his descendants. God proclaimed the Hebrews his "chosen people" and commanded them to worship no other deities.

The first recorded oppression of the Jews occurred about 1,300 years later, when they were enslaved by the Egyptian pharaoh Ramses II. According to the Torah (the first five books of Jewish scripture, which contain Jewish law), after the pharaoh commanded that all male Hebrew newborns be killed, an infant Moses was found by the pharaoh's daughter along the banks of the Nile River. Moses was raised as an Egyptian, but he eventually became the leader of the Hebrews (called Israelites) and successfully led them from bondage. The Israelites wandered in the desert for 40 years before reaching Canaan— the "Promised Land" pledged to Abraham. Before they arrived, Moses received a list of 10 commandments from God—the laws by which the Israelites were to live.

The Israelites eventually established their new nation in Canaan, and their second king, David, who lived during the 11th to 10th centuries B.C., conquered the city of Jerusalem and made it the capital of Israel. For more than 400 years, the Jews flourished in their homeland and kept their covenant with God by offering animal sacrifices and following the Ten Commandments.

In 586 B.C., however, King Nebuchadnezzar II of Babylonia (in present-day Iraq) ordered the attack and destruction of Jerusalem and drove the Israelites out of their homeland. The Israelites spent a generation in exile in Babylonia before Cyrus the Great of Persia, who had conquered Babylonia, permitted them to return around the year 539. Less than 100 years after the city walls were rebuilt, in 333 B.C., Jerusalem was taken from the Persians by Alexander the Great of Macedonia; in 63 B.C. it was conquered by the Roman general Pompey. In A.D. 70, about 40 years after Jesus' death in Jerusalem, the Roman Empire responded to a Jewish revolt by completely destroying the city and the sacred temple. Some of the Jews who chose to resist retreated to a rock fortress known as Masada, where they held off the Romans for three years. When defeat seemed inevitable, they committed suicide.

Once again, the Jewish people were without a nation. Political compromise seemed the only way for them to maintain their spiritual survival, so shortly after the destruction of Jerusalem a rabbi named Yochanan Ben Zakkai forged an agreement with the victorious Roman general Vespasian. The Jews were allowed to occupy a small town called Yavneh, outside Jerusalem. Though they had to relinquish their political independence, they were able to continue studying the Torah and practicing their

faith. This marked a significant shift in the Jewish way of life. No longer did Jews have their own country, with the temple as the center of religious and sacrificial worship.

The birth of Jesus of Nazareth a few decades earlier had forever changed how the rest of the world would view the Jewish people. Old Testament scriptures include the prophet Isaiah's foretelling that God would send a Messiah ("Anointed One") to restore the homeland of the Jews. The arrival of the Messiah, it was prophesied, would also mark the beginning of a magnificent age of peace and holiness for the Jewish people. As Jesus preached to crowds of followers, some Jews came to believe that he was the Anointed One that God had promised.

Jesus presented himself as a "suffering servant" of God, sent to deliver humanity from spiritual death. The Jews believed that their Messiah would be a political deliverer, however. As a result, many Jews rejected Jesus. But because some Jews embraced him as their Messiah—and

In this Renaissance fresco the Babylonian king Nebuchadnezzar, who conquered the Israelites and drove them from their homeland to Babylon in the sixth century B.C., orders the condemnation of some of his Jewish captives. Exile, particularly as an unwelcome or oppressed minority living in foreign lands, is a thread that runs through more than three millennia of Jewish history.

because Jesus inflamed the Scribes and the Pharisees (Hebrew teachers and recorders of the law) by challenging their legitimacy—a split arose among the Jewish people.

Ultimately, Jesus was betrayed by his apostle Judas Iscariot, who had conspired with Jewish authorities to have Jesus arrested. In turn, the Jewish authorities handed him over to the Roman governor, Pontius Pilate, who ordered Jesus' execution. When the tomb in which he had been buried was discovered to be empty, his followers believed that he had risen from the dead, just as he had once prophesied. From this belief, and from the teachings of Jesus—which were spread by his apostles—Christianity was born. The new religion was based on the belief that Jesus was the Messiah his people had hoped for, the Son of God whose death had redeemed sinful humankind.

Although Jesus died at the hands of Roman rulers, many blamed his death on the Jewish authorities who had turned him over to Pontius Pilate. As time passed, this belief fostered among some Christians a resentment of—even a hatred toward—Jews. Christianity became a unifying cultural force in Europe during the period known as the Middle Ages, which is dated from the fall of the Roman Empire in the 5th century to roughly the 15th century. Economic, political, and military ideals were commonly fused with Christian beliefs, spawning institutions such as the Holy Roman Empire, a "revival" of the Roman Empire in western Europe by German rulers who believed themselves legitimate Christian successors of the Romans.

During the Middle Ages it was common for Jews to be vilified as the killers of Jesus, and as Christianity flourished, persecution of the Jews escalated. The Christians who allowed and even promoted this treatment believed the misery that had befallen the Jews was a just punishment from God, not only for having killed Jesus but also for having refused to accept him as their Messiah.

At the end of the 11th century, European Christians launched the first in a two-centuries-long series of religious wars known as the Crusades. The primary objective of the Crusades was to wrest control of the Holy Land (Jerusalem and other biblically significant areas of Palestine) from the Muslims and to establish and defend Christian rule there. But after the successful conquest of Jerusalem in 1099, Crusaders massacred not only the Muslims but also the Jews living in and around the city. As the zeal for extending Christianity intensified, Jews, like Muslims, came to be viewed as enemies of the Christian faith. And Jews often had only one choice: conversion to Christianity or execution. Perhaps no other era in Jewish history matched the persecution and wholesale massacres of this oppressive period—until the Holocaust in the 20th century.

In addition to the old characterizations of Jews as the enemies of God and murderers of Jesus, many Christian leaders during the Middle Ages accused Jews of consorting with Satan and vilified them as parasites living among the righteous. Jews were easy scapegoats for many of society's ills; often they were accused of deliberate acts of evil, such as poisoning the water supply to cause the spread of the Black Death (the bubonic plague that swept Europe and parts of Asia during the 1300s).

In the 15th century, Constantine XI declared Christianity the official religion of the Byzantine Empire. When Constantine mandated that all Jews be converted, they naturally resisted. In response, he applied pressure by enacting laws against them. One such law revoked their citizenship; other laws relegated Jews to the lowest rungs of society by forbidding them to own land or join craft guilds. Left with few options, many Jews became trade merchants, and because the empire forbade Christians to collect interest on loans, Jews also turned to money lending. Although the Church eventually allowed Christians to engage in finance, the Jews who prospered from these businesses were deeply resented and perceived as greedy and ruthless. (An example of this attitude appears in William Shakespeare's play *The Merchant of Venice,* in which the title character is a miserly Jew named Shylock.)

Country after country expelled Jews, often after their usefulness as financiers had been exhausted: Jews were driven out of England in 1290 (and not readmitted until 1655) and forced out of France in 1306. In Spain, beginning in 1478, Jews faced a new and virulent form of persecution: the Spanish Inquisition. The sole purpose of the tribunal, established by the Catholic monarchs King Ferdinand V and Queen Isabella I, was to punish converted Jews and Muslims who appeared to embrace Christianity but who secretly continued to follow their own faith. Various methods of torture were used to extract confessions from those already deemed guilty. Those who continued to profess their innocence were burned alive. Before the end of the 15th century, all Jews had been expelled from Spain. Thousands of them headed into eastern Europe; others sailed for the New World. The *Marranos* (outwardly Christianized Jews who continued to practice the Jewish faith in secret) fled to Portugal, and when an Inquisition was established there, they fled again to Turkey, Italy, and France.

In the 16th century, a new flame of hatred against Jews was ignited, this time in part by the German religious reformer Martin Luther. Luther had taken the Catholic Church to task for its corrupt practice of selling indulgences (remissions of punishment for sin); though condemned by the pope, he refused to retract his objections. Ultimately Luther's followers and other like-minded reformers split with the Catholic Church and created Protestantism.

Trial scene from William Shakespeare's play *The Merchant of Venice*, during which Shylock, the evil, covetous Jewish money-lender, seeks to cut a pound of flesh from a debtor. Because the Catholic Church prohibited its members from charging interest on loans, Jews fulfilled the vital commercial roles of financiers and money-lenders—and in the process earned the stereotype of greedy exploiters.

Though once a supporter of Jews, Luther quickly turned on them when they refused to embrace Protestantism. Perhaps only Adolf Hitler's words exceed Luther's own hateful rhetoric, which offered this suggestion for dealing with Judaism: "to set fire to their synagogues and schools, and to bury and cover with dirt whatever will not burn so that no man will ever again see a stone or a cinder to them." From the 16th century, Jews were forced by law in many European cities to live in separate areas called ghettos.

The 18th century marks what is often called the Age of Reason in Europe. Scientific and intellectual advances in the 17th century had fostered a belief in approaching

Protestant reformer Martin Luther, like many other Christian religious figures, displayed a strong anti-Semitic streak. Luther's prescription for dealing with the Jews was "to set fire to their synagogues and schools, and to bury and cover with dirt whatever will not burn."

Engraved by C.E.Wagstaff.

LUTHER.

From the original Picture by Holbein in his Majesty's Collection at Windsor.

Under the Superintendance of the Society for the Diffusion of Useful Knowledge.

political and social issues from a scientific point of view. Most western European thinkers also subscribed to the theory of "natural law," the conviction that some laws are fundamental to human nature and are discoverable by human reason, rather than by reference to human-made laws, which are formed by history and subject to change.

This liberal thinking slightly improved the position of Jews in European society. For example, in the Austro-Hungarian Empire, Jews were permitted to own land, and after the French Revolution the Jews in France were extended the same "rights of man" as other citizens. Still, European Jews were widely encouraged to forsake their religion and adopt Christianity. In *The World Must Know,* Michael Berenbaum describes the contradiction between the 18th-century ideal of liberty for all and the commonly held antipathy toward Jews as a whole: "To the Jews as individuals, everything," he writes, "to the Jews as a people, nothing."

In the 19th century, many European Jews in search of an accepting country found Germany particularly appealing. A cosmopolitan country, Germany fostered intellectualism and encouraged the fine arts. Still, discrimination was not completely absent. While some of the Jews who settled in Germany continued to practice their religious and cultural traditions, others relinquished them—or even converted to Christianity—in an attempt to assimilate.

The 19th century brought an upsurge of nationalism to Europe, and with it a number of unscientific theories on race that fostered new resentments toward Jews. The word *anti-Semitism* was coined in 1879 by the German nationalist Wilhelm Marr, who despised Jews and incorrectly identified them as a race. In fact, being Jewish was, and is, a religious affiliation, not an element of race or nationality. The word *Semitic* originally referred not to a people but to a group of languages, including Hebrew, Arabic, and Maltese. "Semites" were ethnically based peoples—Arabs, Syrians, and Ethiopians—who came primarily from North Africa and the Middle East. Eventually, however, the term *anti-Semitism* became synonymous with the prevailing negative sentiments against Jews.

Anti-Semitism grew especially strong in Austria, France, and Germany. As Germany struggled with economic problems, anti-Semitic rhetoric became a handy political tool employed by unscrupulous politicians to gain popular support. By exploiting anti-Semitic feelings, the politically ambitious deflected blame for economic and political problems from the government to the Jews. In this social atmosphere, anti-Semitism no longer had to do with a conflict of religious beliefs—it became a means to view Jews as an inferior class of people, who preyed on the well-being of countries and communities where they did not belong and where they were not welcome. The most masterful exploiter of anti-Semitic sentiment was Adolf Hitler, who whipped an entire nation into a frenzy with his vitriolic rhetoric.

Before Hitler took power, 9 million Jews lived in about 21 European countries. Many were professionals—distinguished doctors, lawyers, teachers, businessmen, bankers, and scientists. Others were artists, musicians, writers, designers, and architects. Most were average workers who earned decent incomes and raised their children in modest homes. They included carpenters in Poland; shopkeepers in small, family-owned businesses in France; farmers in Romania; and longshoremen in Greece.

Six hundred years after the Byzantine Empire imposed laws against Jews, Adolf Hitler once more took away their rights as citizens by enacting the Nuremberg Laws. In Milton Meltzer's *Never to Forget,* Holocaust historian Raul Hilberg starkly outlines the progression of centuries of Jewish persecution that culminated in the Holocaust. "The missionaries of Christianity had said in effect: You have no right to live among us as Jews. The secular rulers who followed had proclaimed: You have no right to live among us. The German Nazis at last decreed: You have no right to live." Within 12 years,

The title page of a 1917 anti-Semitic novel published in Leipzig, Germany, depicts the Jew as a vulture ready to feed on a dying German victim.

Hitler saw that millions of these ordinary people—scholars, artists, shopkeepers, homeowners, parents, and children—were dead, murdered for no reason other than that they were Jewish.

Adolf Hitler, photographed during the Weimar Republic period, when his Nazi Party was attempting to build a following through nationalistic, anti-Communist, and anti-Jewish rhetoric.

The Architect of Genocide

"Men are not created equal. As the most superior race on earth, Germans are true creators of culture. Since only they are capable of solving mankind's future problems, the future of civilization depends on them. Therefore, Aryan blood must be kept pure, or these superior qualities will be lost. Marriages to inferior races are forbidden. Germans must create a pure master race to rule the world."

—Adolf Hitler, *Mein Kampf* (1925–27)

Ironically, the hatemonger who proclaimed the need to keep Aryan blood "pure" and who railed against the "inferior" Jews may have himself been part Jewish. Questions have long existed about the identity of Adolf Hitler's paternal grandfather. Hitler's father, Alois Hitler, was the

Adolf Hitler's parents. Above: Alois Hitler, an Austrian civil servant, was a stern disciplinarian. Facing page: Klara Pölzl Hitler doted on and over-indulged her son Adolf.

illegitimate child of Maria Anna Schicklgruber. Maria worked as a cook for the Frankenbergers, a well-to-do Jewish family, in Austria. Some historians speculate that Alois's father was the Frankenbergers' 19-year-old son. If true, that would make Adolf Hitler one-quarter Jewish.

Maria eventually married a millworker named Johann Georg Hiedler, but she died shortly after her wedding. Alois, left in the care of Hiedler, was sent off to a farm with one of Hiedler's brothers. At age 13 he left the farm for Vienna, Austria. Despite a limited education and modest means, he eventually achieved prominence as a customs official in the Austrian government. Proud of his nephew's accomplishments, Alois's uncle convinced him to change his last name to Hiedler. When the name was officially registered, however, it was misspelled and recorded as Hitler.

Alois had been married twice before he met Klara Pölzl, the 24-year-old granddaughter of his uncle. At age 48, he married Klara, and the couple settled in the small Austrian village of Braunau-am-Inn, just across the border from Bavaria. Klara had two miscarriages in three years before she gave birth to a son, Adolf, on April 20, 1889.

Klara was overly protective of her son. She showered him with affection and attention, and Adolf in turn developed a devoted attachment to his mother. Alois, however, was a strict disciplinarian who ran his household in the same regimented manner as he did his civil service job. His demeanor did not soften with his two other children, Edmund, born in 1893, and Paula, born in 1896.

When Adolf was five years old, the Hitler family moved to Leonding, a small town along the Danube River. Despite the importance Alois placed on education, his eldest son did not care much for schooling. He was more interested in drawing and sketching than in his studies. Although not a particularly spirited child, Hitler was captivated by glorious tales of war. He constantly read books on famous battles, and he became obsessed with the Franco-Prussian War of 1870–71, during which a German coalition decisively defeated France. Years later, in his book *Mein Kampf* (My Struggle), a combination of autobiography and political philosophy, Hitler explained how his childhood fascination with that war had profoundly affected him: "It was not long before the great historic struggle had become my greatest spiritual experience," he wrote. "From then on, I became more and more enthusiastic about everything that was in any way connected with war, or for that matter, with soldiering."

By the time Hitler was ready to begin the ninth grade, he had become a rather sullen and spoiled youngster whose only academic interest was in the arts. His father would not allow Hitler to study fine arts, however, and he sent his son to technical school to learn a

The 14-year-old Hitler is in the top row at the far right in this high school class photo. A poor student, he would drop out by age 16.

trade. In defiance, Hitler spent much of his class time doodling and sketching; not surprisingly, he received poor grades. Alois Hitler thought his son was simply lazy and unmotivated. One of Hitler's teachers, on the other hand, described the boy as "notoriously cantankerous, willful, arrogant, and bad tempered."

The struggle between father and son ended with Alois's death in 1903. Adolf Hitler was 14. His mother was not the disciplinarian her husband had been, and Hitler continued to flounder in his studies for the next two years, failing mathematics and German before dropping out of school at age 16.

Without a high school diploma, the future seemed bleak for Adolf Hitler. He was not concerned, however; Alois's substantial pension was enough to support the family comfortably even if his eldest son did not get a job. In the two years after he dropped out of school, Hitler devoted most of his time to sketching and watercolor painting. Never outgoing, he became even more of a loner. He did have one friend, however—a young man named Gustl Kuizek, also a dropout. With Kuizek, Hitler began to discover his skill as an orator. He delivered impassioned speeches on a number of topics, and Kuizek served as his eager audience. Years later, Gustl Kuizek would say of Hitler's talent, "It was not what he said that first attracted me to him, but how he said it."

When Hitler turned 18 in 1907, he received his share of the inheritance left by his father. The sum was substantial enough to support him comfortably for some time. Hitler had become bored with small-town life, and even though his mother had developed cancer, he was determined to leave Leonding. He set his sights on Vienna, Austria's capital, a sophisticated city teeming with art, music, and literature and filled with a mix of people from many classes and backgrounds.

Hitler's main interest in Vienna was the city's renowned Academy of Fine Art. Freed from his father's insistence that he learn a trade, he applied for admittance to the academy to study art. Buoyed by the prospects of a fresh beginning in Vienna, the normally sullen young man became filled with an almost joyous enthusiasm. It did not last long.

Hitler had never considered the possibility that he would be turned down by the Academy of Fine Art. Devastated by the rejection, he now saw life in Vienna as bleak. Worse, the news from Leonding was not good: his mother was losing her battle with cancer. Hitler returned home, and a few days before Christmas, Klara quietly passed away. Years later, her physician recalled the day he went to the Hitler house to sign the death certificate: "In all my career, I never saw anyone so prostrate with grief as Adolf Hitler."

After settling his mother's affairs, Hitler returned to Vienna and reapplied to the Academy of Fine Art. Again, his application was turned down because his work showed little artistic promise. Hitler felt life closing in around him. The death of his mother and the academy's double rejection were more than he could bear. Depressed and frustrated, with no real focus, Hitler squandered his inheritance and was soon living like a vagabond. Often homeless, he slept on park benches and occasionally visited a Viennese soup kitchen for food. He took odd jobs to earn cash, loading luggage at the train station, shoveling snow, or selling his sketches and watercolors to patrons of local taverns.

Hitler had no close friends during this period. He didn't date, smoke, or drink alcohol. His main comfort was the opera. He would always make sure he had enough money to buy a ticket to the newest performance. Hitler loved everything about the opera. In the dark theater, he forgot his troubles and felt swept away by the theatrics and the music. His favorite composer was Richard Wagner, a German whose larger-than-life stage operas were epic tales that glorified his native country.

In 1910, Hitler moved into a boardinghouse for indigent men. When he wasn't wandering the city streets, he would discuss politics with anyone who cared to listen. He developed a passion for reading and borrowed books on German history and mythology from the local library. He also read works by the German philosophers Friedrich Nietzsche, Georg Hegel, and Johann Fichte. It is believed that Hitler's first introduction to anti-Semitic rhetoric came from the writings of the German historian Heinrich von Treitschke, a fanatic nationalist and virulent anti-Semite who wrote the *History of Germany in the Nineteenth Century* (1879–94).

A watercolor painted by Hitler during his vagabond days in Vienna. Though he longed to be a professional artist, he apparently lacked the talent: twice Vienna's prestigious Academy of Fine Art rejected the future dictator's application for admittance.

Another major influence on Hitler's political views was Karl Lueger, an avowed anti-Semite who was mayor of Vienna during the years Hitler lived there. Lueger and racial theorists like Lanz von Liebenfels and Georg von Schoenerer happily blamed Jews for the chaos, corruption, and despair that pervaded life in turn-of-the-century Europe. After all, they declared, it was the Jews who used political and economic manipulation to undermine the once-great German nation and who threatened the very existence of its racial purity. Strongly influenced by these historians, philosophers, and politicians—and hardened by his hand-to-mouth existence—Hitler gradually developed a contempt for Jews, socialists, capitalists, liberals, and other groups that these "experts" claimed were undermining German supremacy.

In 1913, Hitler left Vienna and moved to Munich, Germany, primarily to avoid being drafted into the Austrian military. He would soon have the opportunity to demonstrate his loyalty to his adopted homeland, however.

On June 28, 1914, Archduke Franz Ferdinand, the heir to the Austrian throne, and his wife were assassinated by a Serb radical in Sarajevo, Bosnia. A month later, Austria-Hungary declared war on Serbia. Soon treaty obligations and territorial ambitions had drawn Europe's major powers into the conflict. World War I had begun.

In *Mein Kampf*, Hitler described his reaction upon hearing the news of the war: "Overcome with rapturous enthusiasm, I fell on my knees and thanked Heaven from an overflowing heart for granting me the good fortune of being allowed to live at this time." Why such a joyous reaction to a war? Hitler had been living in poverty, without a home, family, career, or goal. The war gave him a sense of purpose, a feeling that he belonged to some larger cause. Adolf Hitler volunteered for military service.

Hitler became a private with the Sixteenth Bavarian Reserve Infantry Regiment. By most accounts he was a capable soldier. He served as a dispatch runner, carrying messages from military command to officers on the front lines.

World War I was a conflict of unprecedented misery, suffering, destruction, and death, but the horrors Hitler witnessed did not seem to affect him greatly, as they did other soldiers. Although he advanced no higher than the rank of corporal, he was twice awarded the Iron Cross for

bravery and dedication to service. He never complained about conditions and was always willing to volunteer for dangerous assignments. Hitler's high morale stemmed from his complete devotion to the cause of defending the Fatherland. But for him this meant more than simply repelling the armies of France, Great Britain, and the other Allies; the war, Hitler believed, was also a struggle to free Germany from the racially impure influences that had infested his adopted country.

But by early fall of 1918, after four years of fighting, the war began to go badly for Hitler's beloved Germany. Allied offensives pushed the German armies steadily back on the western front, and defeat became inevitable. Unwilling to accept that Germany was being beaten on

A rally in Vienna soon after the outbreak of World War I. "Overcome with rapturous enthusiasm, I fell on my knees and thanked Heaven from an overflowing heart," Hitler (seen in the inset) recalled of the moment he heard about the war.

the battlefield, Hitler began blaming the subversive tactics of Jews and Communists on the home front.

In October 1918, a British gas shell exploded near Hitler, temporarily blinding him. As he lay in his hospital bed, his mind reeled with a terrible vision of defeat and surrender. His nightmare came true: word filtered through that Kaiser Wilhelm, Germany's emperor, had abdicated the throne and fled the country. And on November 11, Germany signed an armistice, or truce, with the Allies, ending the fighting.

The armistice, unfortunately, didn't require Germany to admit defeat. On the home front, a wave of bitterness swept the German people, who were never informed about how dire Germany's military situation had actually become. Many German citizens would, like Hitler, insist that the army had been "stabbed in the back" by politicians—or, as Hitler claimed, by Communists and Jews.

With the kaiser's abdication, however, Germany had a chance to establish a democratic form of government. The adoption of a constitution in August 1919 created what became known as the Weimar Republic, which had a president and a popularly elected parliament, called the Reichstag.

Unfortunately, Germany's experiment in democracy had already been substantially undermined. The Treaty of Versailles, the peace treaty that officially ended World War I, imposed harsh terms on the defeated Germans. Not only did Germany have to accept blame for starting the war, it also had to relinquish territory to France and Poland and pay reparations to the victorious Allies. In addition, all of Germany's colonies were placed under the protection of a new international peace-keeping organization called the League of Nations. The treaty also limited Germany's armed forces to 100,000 men.

Like many other Germans, Adolf Hitler was enraged

by the terms of the Treaty of Versailles. He vowed that the shameful punishment imposed on Germany would one day be avenged. He was determined to play a part in restoring Germany to its former glory, and he set his sights on establishing a German empire greater and stronger than any the world had ever seen.

The Rise of the Third Reich

Berlin street scene, 1919. Demoralized by its defeat in World War I and plagued by inflation, unemployment, and despair, Germany would prove fertile ground for the Nazis' message.

"Democracy and majority rule are stupid. The masses are ignorant sheep that need leading by a brilliant statesman. This divinely appointed leader is Adolf Hitler, who will rule the world with a few chosen elite. The Third Reich, or new German Empire, will last a thousand years. It will be a Nazi totalitarian state with total control of government and the lives of all citizens."

—Adolf Hitler, *Mein Kampf*

At the war's end, Adolf Hitler again found himself displaced, this time amid the chaos and anger of a defeated Germany. Before the war, Hitler had few skills: he could read, but his writing was rough and showed his lack of education. He had held only odd jobs and had no business skills. His desire to be an artist had gone unfulfilled. But at least now he had the army. He'd been a pretty good soldier, and the military was the closest thing he had to a home and a purpose. It seemed natural for him to remain in the service.

In 1919, Hitler took on a new set of military duties in Munich, becoming an "education" officer. One of his primary responsibilities was to monitor the activities of members of various political factions in the city. Hitler's own hatred of foreigners, Jews, and Communists made him an ideal choice for the job. Although most of the groups about which he reported were politically harmless, Hitler was to attend their meetings undercover and to report any events or statements of significance.

In September, Hitler was assigned to investigate a small group that called itself the German Workers' Party. The members met in the back room of a local beer hall, a common gathering place for the discontented at that time. When Hitler arrived, a few dozen men were already discussing the state of the "new" Germany. They debated the negative outcome of the war and laid blame for Germany's problems on Jews and Communists. For Hitler, who had already adopted this viewpoint, the talk echoed a familiar theme—that the true Germans were the Aryan "master race," and that by ridding the country of undesirables Aryans could restore Germany to a position of political and ethnic supremacy.

Still, Hitler had heard such utterances many times before. The talk was so unremarkable that he decided this group wasn't even worth reporting. As he was about to leave, however, one of the men began expounding on his belief that Bavaria should secede from Germany. A staunch nationalist who believed that a strong Germany was a united Germany, Hitler

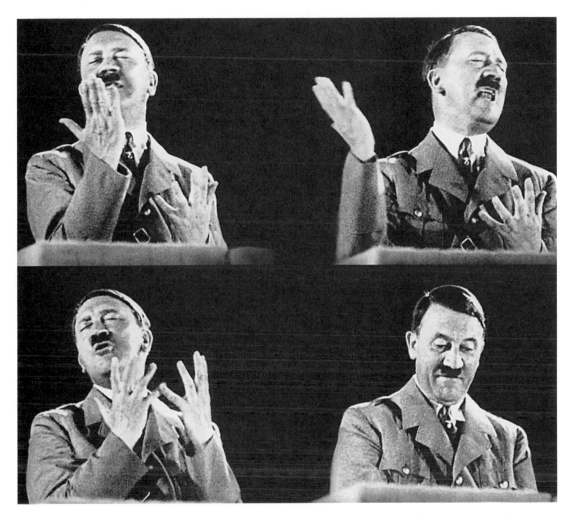

grew enraged. He ranted about how wrong the man was. Since his days at the men's shelter in Vienna, Hitler had steadily improved his oratorical skills— and now his outburst was not only passionate but mesmerizing.

After Hitler had finished, Anton Drexler, the founder of the German Workers' Party, introduced himself and handed Hitler a pamphlet entitled *My Political Awakening*. He was impressed with the new-comer's speech, he said, and he invited Hitler to attend their next meeting.

The demagogue in action: Hitler would rise to leadership in the Nazi Party largely on the strength of his mesmerizing oratory.

Hitler didn't give much thought to the event as he returned to his barracks that evening. The next morning, however, he remembered the pamphlet Drexler had given him, and the more he read the more excited he became. Drexler was describing ideas Hitler himself had—the desire to build a strong political party to reestablish the former empire; the importance of purging the country of inferior races and competing political groups. Just days later, he received an invitation to join the German Workers' Party. Not only did he accept, but he was also elected to the executive committee and charged with promoting the organization. At age 30, with no substantial job experience, Hitler put his failures behind him and entered politics.

On February 24, 1920, before more than 2,000 people gathered in a Munich beer hall, Hitler unveiled the platform of the German Workers' Party. Included in the 25-point program was an outright rejection of the Treaty of Versailles. He also introduced the concept of *Lebensraum*—literally, "living space"—asserting that Germany would be justified in acquiring additional territory to ensure its national survival. Most significantly, perhaps, Hitler suggested that German citizenship be determined by race. For the first time, he was publicly expressing two of his primary objectives: the expansion of Germany, and the exclusion from German society of anyone other than "pure" Germans.

Within two years, the German Workers' Party grew to more than 3,000 members. Some of the newcomers were restless and disgruntled former soldiers. Most came to hear the fever-pitch speeches of the party's gifted orator, Adolf Hitler, and then ended up joining. By 1921, Hitler had transformed a small band of malcontents into a growing political organization.

He assumed leadership of the party and renamed it the National Socialist German Workers' Party, or the Nazi Party for short. He chose a centuries-old symbol of prosperity and good fortune as its emblem: the swastika, a cross with hooked arms. Before long the swastika seemed to be everywhere—on Nazi uniforms, flags, propaganda posters, and buildings. Hitler protected his own increasing authority by enlisting the aid of old army colleagues, who were more than happy to use brute force to silence opposition.

For a disheartened, disgruntled population still struggling to overcome the consequences of World War I, Hitler's message held powerful appeal. He understood their grievances because he had the same complaints and had had many of the same experiences. There were enemies in Germany, he said; there was no doubt about that. The mighty German army had been "stabbed in the back" by traitors, like the Marxists who wanted to turn Germany toward communism. They had been betrayed by their kaiser, who in order to save himself had abdicated and abandoned his people. Finally, they had been betrayed by the Jews, who'd undermined the war effort for their own economic and financial gain.

Plagued by unemployment and runaway inflation, Germany's economy was in dire straits. German pride had been badly bruised. Many people heard Hitler's message and agreed: it was time to fight back.

As the Nazi Party gained momentum, Hitler began gathering a circle of confidants. Among them was a former army captain named Ernst Röhm, whom Hitler charged with establishing a private Nazi army—the *Sturmabteilungen* (Storm Troopers), or SA. These ruthless recruits adopted an ominous looking uniform that included dark brown shirts and knee-high black leather boots. Röhm was backed by a number of politicians concerned about the stability of the democratic Weimar Republic and fearful of a Communist revolution. Seeing the Nazi Party's military force as a reasonable alternative, they gave SA members free rein to attack or kill anyone who openly opposed the party. Before long, the SA was operating completely above the law and had become the most feared organization in Munich.

Many of the men Hitler welcomed into the Nazi Party had been military misfits or fanatics who sought a cause to which they could devote their energies. Among the earliest members were Hermann Göring and Rudolf Hess. Blond, blue-eyed Göring, a World War I hero and educated officer, was considered the ideal Aryan specimen; he brought a fiery zeal to the Nazi Party. Hess, on the other hand, was a lost soul after Germany's military and political defeat. After hearing Hitler speak at a Nazi rally, Hess developed an instant devotion to the party leader.

By 1923 Hitler believed that the time was ripe for his party to overthrow the Weimar regime. Assembling more that 600 SA soldiers, Hitler marched to Munich's Bürgerbräukeller beer hall to commence the revolution. The attempted coup, derisively called the Beer Hall Putsch, failed miserably. Hitler was arrested the next day, but he defended himself before a group of judges that had been selected by a Nazi sympathizer in the Bavarian government. He didn't deny his treasonous actions; rather, he embraced them. The Weimar government was the real criminal, Hitler declared; he was simply a genuine German loyalist. Found guilty of high treason, Hitler nevertheless avoided the standard punishment of life in prison. Instead, he was sentenced to just five years at Landsberg prison. In the end, he was behind bars only nine months.

Hitler used the time well. Having learned the pitfalls of trying to take power by force, he began planning a political revolution. While in Landsberg prison, Hitler wrote his notorious propaganda-filled memoirs, *Mein Kampf*. For the first time, Hitler stated in print what he believed was the root cause of all Germany's ills—namely, the influence of Jews and Communists—and he outlined his program for restoring the country to its rightful place as the world's preeminent nation.

Hitler's utter contempt for Jews is plain in *Mein Kampf*. He scorns them as parasites, liars, cheats, maggots, "eternal blood suckers," destroyers of the Aryan race. Jews, "the most inferior race," Hitler maintains, "are the true destroyers of culture. They have deliberately invaded and drained all countries of the world of money and power. Therefore, the future of world power rests on either the rightful German masters or

Hitler and four co-conspirators do not-so-hard time in Landsberg prison for their role in the 1923 Munich Beer Hall Putsch, an abortive attempt to overthrow the Weimar government. Though treason was punishable under German law by life imprisonment, Hitler received a sentence of only five years—and ended up serving just nine months.

the Jews. Germans must save the world by ridding it of this Jewish poison."

Perhaps unfortunately, the initial publication of *Mein Kampf* in 1925 went almost unnoticed. Had more people read the slight volume written by the relatively unknown political dissident, Germany and the world might have been forewarned of his intentions. For within the pages of *Mein Kampf,* Hitler plainly bares his determination to seize power and rid Germany of Jews.

For his part in the beer hall uprising, Hitler had been banned from public speaking. In addition, the Nazi Party had been declared illegal. Hitler was undeterred, however. After his release from Landsberg, he set out to resurrect the party. Unfortunately for him, the political situation in Germany had stabilized somewhat in the months since the putsch, and many former Nazi enthusiasts had lost interest in a revolution. Still, Hitler didn't give up. With the help of his minister of public enlightenment and propaganda, Joseph Goebbels, and the head of his *Gestapo* (a division of Nazi secret police known especially for brutality), Hermann Göring, Hitler formed a new, elite guard called the *Schutzstaffel* (SS). With this brutal cadre, Hitler began restoring the Nazi Party.

To gain a political foothold in Germany, Hitler assigned Nazi Party members as *gauleiters* (governors or district leaders) in towns throughout the country. In 1927, when the ban against the Nazi Party was lifted, the *gauleiters* began running in local elections in an attempt to capture seats in the Reichstag. It didn't take long: in 1928, the Nazi Party won 12 Reichstag seats.

The Great Depression, which was precipitated by the U.S. stock market crash of 1929, brought new opportunities for the Nazis. As the German economy further disintegrated, frustrated and besieged Germans began hearing the fiery words of Adolf Hitler with renewed interest. Beset by staggering unemployment and high inflation, Germans looked to a leader who could draw them back into prosperity. Hitler, fully aware of the opportunity, broadened his message to appeal to middle-class workers, peasants, small businessmen, conservatives, and industrialists. With each speech he delivered, the Nazi Party gained more followers.

Hitler and the Nazi *gauleiters* campaigned tirelessly in the 1930 national elections. Goebbels carefully orchestrated Hitler's appearances to create a powerful impression. His entrance was always preceded by rows of marching Brownshirts (SA members), and he arrived amid billowing, swastika-adorned Nazi flags and triumphal music. The drama was effective: Nazi candidates received almost 6.4 million votes, which earned them a stunning 107 seats in the Reichstag. Under Hitler's leadership, the Nazi Party had become the second-largest government party in Germany.

Meanwhile, however, the German economy continued to decline. Two years into the Great Depression, 6 million Germans were out of work. More businesses failed every day. The Reichstag, weakened by splintered political groups that left no clear majority, could achieve very little. Now, Hitler decided, was the time to seize the presidency. He decided to run against the incumbent, Paul von Hindenburg, an 85-year-old war hero who had been in office for seven years. Hindenburg was responsible for the little stability Germany enjoyed during the difficult postwar years of the Weimar Republic.

Once more, Hitler campaigned furiously, this time under the potent slogan "Freedom and Bread." In the elections of March 1932, Hindenburg failed to garner

"Adolf Hitler will provide work and bread!" declares the Nazi campaign banner from 1932. The Nazis' success at the polls prompted President Paul von Hindenburg to appoint Hitler to the post of chancellor— a decision that would have catastrophic consequences for Germany and the entire world.

the simple majority required for the presidency, but he did earn a second seven-year term in a runoff election the following month.

Hitler wasn't through yet, however. One of Hindenburg's duties was to appoint a new chancellor (a chief minister or executive officer meant to serve the ruling president). Through heavy political pressure, Hitler maneuvered his way into the post despite Hindenburg's misgivings. On January 30, 1933, Adolf Hitler became Reich Chancellor of Germany. He had finally gained the political power he had long sought.

"The Jews Are Our Misfortune"

Brownshirts block the entrance to a Jewish-owned store in Berlin, April 1, 1933. Though the Nazi-inspired boycott of Jewish businesses collapsed after less than a day, it presaged the progressively more virulent attacks on Jews that culminated in the Holocaust.

"The end of German Jewry has arrived."

—Rabbi Leo Baeck, shortly after Hitler became chancellor of Germany

On the evening of Hitler's appointment as German chancellor, a huge celebration filled the streets of Munich. Hundreds of SA and SS troops marched to the chancellery building to honor their leader. Throngs of soldiers, men, women, and children waited impatiently for Hitler to make a speech. When he finally emerged from the building, the crowd chanted "Victory! Victory!"

Not all Germans were celebrating the occasion. Many felt uneasy about Hitler's rise to power. Hindenburg had even received an ominous telegram from one of Hitler's former supporters, General Erich Ludendorff. Ludendorff, who had joined Hitler in the failed 1923 Beer Hall Putsch, wrote, "By appointing Hitler Chancellor of the Reich, you have handed over our sacred German Fatherland to one of the greatest demagogues of all time. I prophesy to you [that] this evil man will plunge our Reich into the abyss and will inflict immeasurable woe on our nation."

In his new position Hitler immediately began plotting to seize total control of Germany. First, he planned to unseat all members of the Reichstag who opposed the Nazi Party. He called on Hindenburg to dissolve the Reichstag and to hold new elections. Hitler then met with Germany's General Staff to gain the backing of the country's top military leaders. He assured the generals that he wanted to begin rearming and rebuilding the military in defiance of Versailles Treaty restrictions. Eager to protect their own positions and to maintain the influence of the military, the General Staff supported him.

Hitler still needed to find a way to discredit his opposition and consolidate Nazi power. A Communist sympathizer unwittingly gave him his opportunity. On February 27, 1933, a massive inferno engulfed the Reichstag building. A Dutch Communist named Marinus van der Lubbe was charged with having set the fire. In near hysterical tones, Hitler accused the Bolsheviks (Russian Communists) of plotting a revolution to overthrow the German government. He raged that all Communist Party members were the enemies of Germany and should be executed.

The next day, Hitler gathered cabinet members to draft an "emergency decree" called the Law for the Protection of the People and the State. The decree essentially established a police state in Germany. It placed severe restrictions on personal liberties, such as freedom of speech, of the press, and of privacy of mail, telephone, and telegraph communication. It eliminated the requirement that authorities obtain a warrant to conduct house searches, confiscate property, or arrest citizens.

Badly shaken by the fire, a frightened Hindenburg signed Hitler's decree. The mandate unleashed a legal reign of terror in Germany. At Göring's order, hundreds of SA and SS troops stormed into the homes of suspected opposition members, kicking and beating them senseless before dragging them off in the darkness. Within the first six months of Hitler's chancellorship, more than 25,000 German citizens were jailed as traitors.

The new election Hitler had demanded took place on March 5, 1933. Though the Nazis garnered only 43 percent of the vote, support from Nationalist Party members finally gave Hitler a 52 percent majority in the Reichstag. To extend his margin of control in the new Reichstag, Hitler had 81 Communist members removed on the grounds that they were "enemies of the state." Later in the month, the Nazi-controlled legislature passed the Enabling Act, which granted Hitler the authority to enact laws without parliamentary approval. The Enabling Act made the constitution of the Weimar Republic a useless document and gave Hitler dictatorial power. Democracy in Germany was dead.

Hitler now had what he wanted, and he ruled by fear. SA and SS soldiers, fiercely loyal to the chancellor, continued their violent assault against anyone who voiced opposition. Heinrich Himmler's Gestapo infiltrated the lives of ordinary citizens, attempting to gain information on suspected enemies of the state. The most innocent comment or expression of dissatisfaction with Hitler's new government could result in imprisonment. Hitler refused to tolerate disagreement, whether real or imagined.

Nazi officials review SA bicycle troops during a 1933 parade. The Storm Troopers intimidated, beat, and murdered opponents of Hitler's regime in the first months of the Third Reich.

In addition to threats of physical harm, Hitler skillfully employed propaganda to gain the approval—and the fearful respect—of the German people. Joseph Goebbels organized rally after rally in massive displays of the Nazi Party's might. Huge red Nazi flags emblazoned with black swastikas were draped from windows along parade routes, almost cloaking the buildings behind them, as thousands of uniformed soldiers marched through the streets in precision formations, boot heels clacking against the pavement in a single thundering beat. Who dared challenge a regime that could flex that kind of military muscle?

Though a Communist sympathizer had given Hitler the opportunity to seize power, the chancellor had not forgotten the "treachery" of the Jews. His conviction that they were the enemies of Germany had been no secret, and now that he held power he was finally able to act on his beliefs. For years, Hitler had accused Jews of subversive control over Germany. It was the profiteering Jews, he thundered, who had undermined the German effort in World War I. It was the Jews who had manipulated the postwar economy, causing inflation and a depression in an effort to pad their own pockets. It was the Jews, Hitler insisted, who controlled industry and banking and who secretly set pro-Jewish policy in the Weimar government.

In reality, of the 66 million people who lived in Germany in 1933, only 525,000—a mere 1 percent of the population—were Jewish. Moreover, German Jews were among the most assimilated in the world. They heartily embraced German culture, and in the process many had relinquished their own religious practices. They intermarried, and some even changed their names to sound Germanic. As a rule, German Jews were loyal patriots. Of the 100,000 who served in World War I, 80,000 had been on the front lines. Thirty-five thousand received recognition for bravery in battle; more than 12,000 died fighting for Germany. Would a people who merely sought financial profit from a war risk their own lives in such numbers?

Most German Jews were middle-class working people, and when the Great Depression hit Germany, even those who had once been wealthy stood in bread lines with other impoverished Germans. Despite Hitler's insistence that Jews secretly controlled the world's economy, only 2 percent of Germany's bankers and brokers were Jewish. It is true that German Jews flourished in business. Most worked in traditionally Jewish occupations, such as the garment industry. Others sold leather goods, shoes, and jewelry. But the biggest industries—iron and steel, petroleum, and chemical manufacturing—were owned and operated by non-Jewish Germans.

Hitler had often accused the "enemies of the Fatherland" of infiltrating the Weimar government as well, manipulating laws and policies to the detriment of the German people. Was it possible that the 7 Jews in the 260-member Reichstag between 1919 and 1933 could wield that much control? The fact is that Germany's Jews were never part of a conspiracy to exercise economic or political power. They were never a threat to German stability. Instead, they were hard-working, dedicated people—just as most non-Jewish Germans tried to be. They ran businesses, taught in schools, practiced law and medicine, and worked as artists, musicians, engineers, scientists, and journalists. Some achieved exceptional distinction in their fields: of the 38 Nobel Prizes awarded to Germans between 1905 and 1936, 14 were presented to Jews.

None of this mattered to Adolf Hitler. For years, in his speeches, in his writings, and in private conversations, he had vowed to rid Germany of Jews. Now he had the power to fulfill his promise.

No one but Hitler himself could say whether his initial plan to eliminate Jews from Europe included mass murder. From the outset, however, he was extremely vocal about freeing Germany from the Jewish "scourge." At the very least, he hoped to make life so miserable for Jews that they would leave en masse of their own accord.

Between 1933 and 1938, Hitler methodically implemented restrictions meant to strip Jews of their

Julius Lisser.

שר

Fabrik ff Fleisch & Wurst
Waren
mit elektr. Kraftbetrieb

Telephon 786.

Julius Lisser.

"German-ness." He revoked their citizenship, banned them from many occupations, restricted their movements throughout the country, and otherwise ostracized them from German society.

Even before Hitler gained the chancellorship, however, attacks on Jews had been fairly common. Synagogues and Jewish cemeteries were regularly vandalized. Random beatings and even killings sometimes took place as well. When protesting the persecution at home failed to yield results, Jewish community leaders spread news of what was happening to the rest of the world.

Furious over foreign criticism that resulted from such information, Hitler launched a retaliatory attack against German Jews. He met with Goebbels, his propaganda

A kosher butcher shop in Danzig. Although many European Jews maintained their religious and cultural traditions and sought to stay apart from the broader societies in which they lived, many others, particularly in Germany, assimilated. Before the rise of Adolf Hitler, Jews worked in all sectors of the German economy.

minister. "We shall only be able to combat the falsehoods abroad if we get at those who originated them or at those Jews living in Germany who have thus far remained unmolested," Goebbels told Hitler. "We must, therefore, proceed to a large-scale boycott of all Jewish business in Germany. Perhaps the foreign Jews will think better of the matter when their racial comrades in Germany begin to get it in the neck." A few days later, Hitler announced a nationwide boycott of Jewish businesses.

The official boycott began at 10:00 A.M. on April 1, 1933. Storm Troopers roamed Germany's streets, without concern for police intervention. They distributed boycott pamphlets to non-Jews and stood ominously in front of Jewish-owned shops, blocking customers from entering. They held up signs with messages such as "Germans! Defend Yourselves! Don't buy from Jews!" and "The Jews are our Misfortune." They defaced commercial properties by painting the Star of David or the identifying word *Jude* (Jew) on storefront windows and doors of businesses owned by Jews.

The reaction by non-Jewish Germans was mixed. In some cities the Nazi boycott inspired an outbreak of hostility toward German Jews. Others called their Jewish friends to warn them of the danger. Many patronized Jewish businesses in defiance of the boycott, outraged at what they believed was a grave injustice against neighbors and friends. As a result, Hitler's grandly planned boycott, which was supposed to last for five days, quickly died from lack of support, ending the day it began.

The boycott, while unsuccessful, marked the beginning of a relentless assault against Jews by the German government. On April 7, 1933, Hitler announced the first of more than 400 pieces of anti-Jewish legislation that would be passed between 1933 and 1939. The laws not only segregated Jewish people from the rest of German society, but also stripped them of their businesses, their property, and their personal possessions.

A three-law blitz beginning in April 1933 began with the passage of the Restoration of the Professional Civil Service Act. The law, which removed from government jobs all non-Aryans, put more than 28,000 Jewish teachers, judges, lawyers, hospital workers, and others out of work. On April 21, Jews were forbidden to follow their own kosher laws in butchering meat. Four days later, the Reichstag passed the Law Against the Overcrowding of German Schools and Institutions of Higher Learning. This strictly limited the number of non-Aryan students permitted to attend German schools. Jewish families were forced to educate their children in segregated schools.

Hitler and his Nazi Party had other important tasks to complete that year as well. First, they initiated a campaign to remove all literature that hindered the "purification" of German culture. Propaganda Minister Goebbels orchestrated an event that exhilarated Nazi followers but caused panic among many others. On the night of May 10, thousands of Germans, including students, professors, Nazi sympathizers, and party officials, rushed into bookstores, school libraries, and public libraries, seizing books that were written by Jews or were in any way viewed as "un-German." The confiscated books were tossed into huge piles in public view, and then they were torched.

In one city, books arrived by an oxcart that entered the square to Frédéric Chopin's *Funeral March*. The book burners danced and chanted around the massive bonfires. Hundreds of thousands of books were destroyed that night, including works by famed German writers such as the Nobel Prize–winning novelist Thomas Mann, the dramatist and poet Bertolt Brecht, and Erich Maria

The Nazis' May 10, 1933, book-burning rally targeted "un-German" books, including those written by Jews and those deemed to reflect democratic principles.

Remarque, author of the celebrated antiwar novel *All Quiet on the Western Front*. Books by Sigmund Freud, considered the father of psychoanalysis, were destroyed; the Austrian-born Freud was Jewish. Nor were books by such renowned non-Jewish American writers as Ernest Hemingway, Jack London, Sinclair Lewis, and Helen Keller spared.

Ironically, a century before this destruction, a German Jewish poet named Heinrich Heine had unknowingly prophesied the event—and its chilling outcome. "Where one burns books," Heine wrote, "one will, in the end, burn people." Only eight years passed, Holocaust historian Michael Berenbaum points out, between the time Germany began burning books and the time it began incinerating its own citizens.

In all, Hitler had 42 anti-Jewish laws enacted during his first year as chancellor of Germany. Many Jews hoped that the Nazi Party's oppressive policies would end there. Others believed that it was time to go elsewhere, before conditions worsened. By the end of 1933, more than 37,000 German Jews—about 7 percent of the country's Jewish population—had fled Germany. But that number was unacceptable to Hitler, who had hoped Jews would leave Germany en masse. To convince the remaining Jews that they were unwelcome, he would have to become more repressive and unleash even more violence.

"Juden Verboten"

"Jews are not desired here," reads the sign above an entrance to the University of Erlangen. As the 1930s wore on, the Nazis increasingly shut Jews out of the academic, cultural, and commercial life of Germany.

"Dead silence—not a sound to be heard in town. The lamps in the street, the lights in the shops and in the houses are out. It is 3:30 A.M. All of a sudden noises in the street break into my sleep, a wild medley of shouts and shrieks. I listen, frightened and alarmed, until I distinguish words: "Get out, Jews! Death to the Jews."

—Holocaust survivor Norman Bentwich

The onslaught of anti-Semitic legislation enacted in 1933 virtually ensured that Jews would be removed from the mainstream of German society. Legally sanctioned discrimination against the Jews also encouraged private citizens across the country to publicly voice their disdain for Jews. Signs reading *"Juden Verboten"* (Jews Forbidden) appeared in shop windows and other public places. Julius Streicher, the rabidly anti-Semitic editor of *Der Stürmer*, fanned the flames of bigotry by printing a constant stream of verbal assaults against, and vicious caricatures of, Jews in his weekly newspaper.

Hitler's grand plan for Germany went far beyond simply resolving "the Jewish problem," however. In the spring of 1933, as the first of the anti-Jewish laws were being enacted, Germany's first concentration camp opened in Dachau. Few people noticed. Dachau's purpose was to incarcerate political prisoners of the Nazi regime. But SS leader Heinrich Himmler soon realized that concentration camp prisoners provided an abundant source of slave labor, and Dachau would serve as a model for many other concentration camps constructed over the next decade.

Hitler's quest to fashion a racially pure Germany went hand-in-hand with his policy of *Lebensraum*, obtaining more living space for Germans. He planned to seize territory from other European countries. Ignoring the terms of the Treaty of Versailles, which forbade Germany to maintain a submarine or military aircraft fleet and restricted its ground forces to 100,000 soldiers, Hitler set about rebuilding the country's military. To punctuate his disdain for the treaty, he withdrew Germany from arms talks sponsored by the League of Nations, which had been ongoing for more than a year in Geneva, Switzerland. On October 21, 1933, Hitler withdrew Germany from the League of Nations altogether.

Around this time, Hitler encountered a troublesome problem within his own party. Led by Ernst Röhm, the Brownshirts had surged in strength to more than 4 million members, and when rumblings of discontent over Hitler's policies arose among the SA leadership, the chancellor took swift action. On June 30, 1934, during what came to be called "the Night of Long Knives," more than 1,000 SA

members were rounded up and executed. In explaining the slaughter, Hitler claimed that while regrettable, it had been necessary to suppress acts of treason against Germany.

A month later, on August 2, Hitler finally grasped what he viewed as the ultimate prize—total control over Germany—after the ailing president, Paul von Hindenburg, died. Within hours of the president's death, Hitler issued a decree that unified the positions of chancellor and president and named himself *Führer* ("leader" or "guide"). By his own proclamation, Hitler became not only the head of state of Germany, but also the commander-in-chief of its armed forces.

Because no anti-Semitic legislation had been passed in 1934, and because Hitler had purged the SA of some of its most ruthless leaders, German Jews hoped that the worst had passed. But Hitler had only begun his assault. The 1933 laws forbidding Jews to hold or practice certain occupations restricted them from fully participating in German society.

Inmates at Dachau, 1934. Germany's first concentration camp, Dachau was constructed to incarcerate political dissidents. But Nazi officials soon recognized the value of slave labor in producing goods for the war economy, and they came to see concentration camps as a possible solution to "the Jewish problem."

The second wave of anti-Jewish laws, however, would attack Jews as a people.

Hitler and his propaganda minister were fond of staging elaborate, celebratory rallies each year in the city of Nuremberg, the industrial center of Germany and the site of several armaments factories. In the chancellor's eyes, the 1934 rally was a masterpiece (it has been preserved by the controversial filmmaker Leni Riefenstahl in her documentary *Triumph of the Will*). The following year, the festivities were climaxed by Hitler's announcement of two new laws that specifically targeted Jews. These laws, known as the 1935 Nuremberg Race Laws (or simply the Nuremberg Laws), became the nucleus of Hitler's anti-Semitic decrees. The first, known as the Reich Citizenship Law, stripped Jews of citizenship and made them "subjects" of Germany. They were no longer permitted to vote, serve in the military, or hold public office. Another decree, the Law for the Protection of German Blood and German Honor, was a means to ensure racial purity in Germany: it forbade Jews to marry or have sexual relations with "citizens of German or kindred blood."

In all, 13 decrees were added to the Nuremberg Laws. They included segregating Jews on public transportation and in public waiting areas; forbidding them to use public beaches, vacation resorts, or baths; and imposing a daily 8:00 P.M. curfew, by which time all Jews were required to be off the streets. Private telephones were removed from Jewish homes, and later Jews were also forbidden to use public telephones.

Hitler argued that these restrictions were simply a reinstatement of government laws in place before the "liberalization" of Germany. Milton Meltzer, in his book *Never to Forget*, cites a Nazi Party member's summary of Hitler's intentions when he established the anti-Semitic laws: "It will henceforth and for all future times be impossible for the

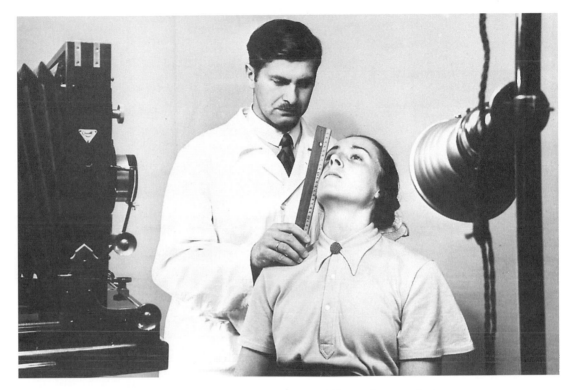

Jews to mix with the German people and to meddle in the political, economic, and cultural management of the Reich."

The Nuremberg Laws forced the Nazis to define what being a Jew meant. They classified Jews in two categories: "full Jews," those having at least three Jewish grandparents, and "*Mischlinge*" (mongrels), those who were only partly of Jewish descent. The second category was then subdivided into "First-Class *Mischlinge*," those with two Jewish grandparents who did not practice the religion and were not married to Jews, and "Second-Class *Mischlinge*," those with only one Jewish grandparent.

The tortuous classification system left one fact clear: anyone who had a Jewish grandparent was Jewish, and was therefore stripped of all German citizenship rights. For the first time in Jewish history, Jews were persecuted not because of their religious beliefs but because of their supposed racial identity.

A doctor measures a German woman's facial features. Nazi pseudo-science attempted to identify the physical characteristics of the supposedly superior Aryan "race." Nazi laws attempted to keep Aryans genetically "pure."

The government sanctions inspired renewed persecution and discrimination from non-Jewish Germans. More businesses openly posted *Juden Verboten* or *Juden Unerwünscht* (Jews Unwelcome) signs on storefronts, in restaurants and theaters, and in pharmacies. Although Nazi officials delighted in the effectiveness of their anti-Semitic campaign, Hitler knew that he needed to downplay his decrees against Jews when the 1936 Olympic Games came to Germany. The world's eyes would be on the Fatherland, and he intended to prove to all that the "new" Germany was a powerful and prosperous nation.

The Olympics (the Summer Games were held in Berlin; the Winter Games in Garmisch-Partenkirchen) also provided the perfect opportunity for Hitler to display what he believed were Germany's racially and physically superior Aryan athletes. Jewish athletes had long been forbidden to participate in sports clubs and national competitions, and none were on Germany's Olympic teams. A few countries threatened to boycott the 1936 Olympic Games, claiming that the host country had violated the Olympic prohibition against discrimination by class, religion, or race. In the end, however, no one stayed away. The decision may seem faint-hearted, but in countries such as the United States, it was motivated at least in part by good intentions. Many feared that a U.S. boycott might trigger even greater oppression of German Jews. Moreover, Hitler suspended his anti-Jewish campaign during the Olympics.

After the Olympics, Hitler turned his attention to *Lebensraum.* In the fall of 1937, he told his state and military officers that he planned to acquire Czechoslovakia and his birthplace, Austria. The prospect seemed outrageous: he intended to annex two European countries. Hitler seemed untroubled by the threat of international interference—and with good reason. In 1936, he had reoccupied the Rhineland, a western region along the Rhine River that the

Treaty of Versailles had prohibited Germany from entering. No other countries objected to the reoccupation. That same year, he had hosted an Olympic Games that no country boycotted, despite widespread accusations of German persecution of Jews.

The suspension of anti-Semitic laws during the Olympic Games was the final reprieve for Jews in Germany. By the end of 1937, more than 130,000 of them had fled the country in terror. Because it was difficult to leave Europe, most of the émigrés settled in Belgium, Czechoslovakia, France, the Netherlands, and Great Britain. Still, more than 75 percent of Germany's Jews remained within its borders—and when Hitler achieved *Anschluss* (political union) with Austria on March 13, 1938, he inherited its Jewish population, which exceeded 200,000. Hitler now had to contend with approximately 600,000 Jews.

Most of Austria's Jews lived in Vienna, the city that Hitler had once roamed as a vagabond. Yet no sentimentalism prevented him from acting immediately to enforce anti-Semitic decrees. Germany had no sooner annexed Austria than its Jewish population was oppressed, humiliated, even physically attacked. Jewish men had their beards (a sign of their reverence for God) shorn in front of mocking crowds. Jewish men and women were ordered to their hands and knees to scrub sidewalks and streets. Some were coerced into defacing their own shops by painting the word *Jude* on the facades.

Shortly after the *Anschluss*, the SS division of the Gestapo was put in charge of handling Jewish affairs. As overseer of the new Office for Jewish Emigration, Adolf Eichmann, a Nazi Security Service (SD) leader and "Jewish expert," was charged with overseeing the "resettlement" of Austrian (and later, Czechoslovakian) Jews. It was Eichmann who later implemented the forced evacuation, registration, and deportation of millions of Jews to the death camps.

Jewish men are forced to scrub the pavement as Austrian police and Viennese residents look on with amusement. Public humiliations of Austrian Jews began almost immediately after the *Anschluss*, Germany's 1938 unification with Austria.

The mass emigrations of German Jews did not go unnoticed by the rest of the world. More and more Jews attempting to escape Nazi oppression looked to other countries for refuge. Eleven days after the *Anschluss*, U.S. president Franklin D. Roosevelt called for an international conference to address the problem and find ways for other nations to accommodate the Jewish emigrants. Delegates from 32 countries in Europe, North America, Latin America, and Australia and New Zealand met at the resort town of Evian-les-Bains, France. For nine days, from July 6 to 15, 1938, delegates rose one by one and spoke in sympathetic tones about the German refugee problem—but all invariably followed with reasons why their country could not accept additional Jewish refugees. Nearly all of them had immigration quotas that they were reluctant to change, despite the dire situation in Germany. Only the tiny Caribbean nation of the Dominican Republic stepped forward, offering to take in 100,000 Jews.

Hitler reveled in the failure of the Evian Conference. He had the German Foreign Office release a gloating statement: "Since in many countries it was recently regarded as wholly incomprehensible why Germany did not wish to preserve in its population an element like the Jews," the statement read, "it appears astounding that countries seem in no way anxious to make use of these elements themselves now that the opportunity offers." What the delegates to the Evian Conference did not realize was that their failure sealed the fate of millions of Jews, who were now trapped in the Nazi sphere of influence. The results of the conference sent a clear message to Adolf Hitler: no one wanted the Jews, and forced emigration would not rid Germany of them.

Still, Hitler continued trying to compel Jews to leave Germany. In 1938 he unleashed another barrage of restrictions. In April, Jews were ordered to register their wealth and personal property with the German government; shortly thereafter, all Jewish-owned businesses were required to be registered. At the end of July, all Jews age 15 and older were issued identity cards that they had to produce upon the order of any German police officer. In August, as a sign of their heritage, all Jewish men were required to add "Israel" and women to add "Sarah" to their own names on all legal documents.

The *Lebensraum* policy continued as well. In September 1938, Germany signed an agreement with Great Britain, France, and Italy that ceded the Sudetenland, an area of Czechoslovakia, to Germany. With the Munich Pact, Hitler had gained 3.5 million German-speaking citizens in the Sudetenland. He had also gained 130,000 more Jews. Hitler raged about the growing population of Jews in German-controlled territory.

A July 3, 1938, *New York Times* political cartoon addresses the dilemma of German Jews: while the Nazis wanted them out of Germany, the international community was unwilling to accept them, as the Evian Conference made clear.

As winter approached, life for German Jews became even bleaker. On October 5, all passports issued to Jews were confiscated, and any that were reissued to Jews required the stamp of a large red *J*. In mid-October, the Nazis confiscated Jewish property and investments, including businesses, real estate, stocks and bonds, and anything else of significant value.

The new restrictions were bad enough, but a minor event was about to give the *Führer* an excuse to unleash a new wave of violence against the Jews. On October 28, SD chief Reinhard Heydrich ordered that 12,000 Jews of Polish origin be rounded up, expelled from Germany, and taken to Zbaszyn, a town along the Polish border. By the time Poland agreed to accept them, winter had set in, and the homeless Jews had no choice but to find temporary shelter in makeshift tents, barns, stables, and abandoned shacks. In the harsh winter of eastern Europe, many of them died from exposure, illness, and starvation.

Among the deported Jews were 52-year-old Zindel Grynszpan and his wife. Grynszpan sent a postcard describing their plight to his 17-year-old son, Herschel, who was visiting an uncle in Paris, France. Furious and grief-stricken at the news, Herschel walked into the German embassy in Paris on November 7 and shot the first Nazi official he encountered. His victim, an embassy staffer named Ernst von Rath, died two days later.

For the Nazi government, the incident provided a golden opportunity. The shooter was denounced as a conspirator in a widespread Jewish plot to overthrow the Third Reich. In retaliation, Heydrich and propaganda minister Joseph Goebbels instructed all Nazi regional chiefs to launch an all-out assault against Jews. Thus began the rampage known as *Kristallnacht,* or "Night of Broken Glass." In the next 24 hours, scores of Jews were randomly beaten and murdered, their homes ransacked, and Jewish women and children defiled. American consul David Buffman described with horror the events that took place in the city of Leipzig on *Kristallnacht*:

At 3 A.M. on 10 November 1938 was unleashed a barrage of Nazi ferocity as had no equal hitherto in Germany, or very likely anywhere else in the world since savagery began. Jewish buildings were smashed into and the contents demolished or looted. In one of the Jewish sections, an 18-year-old boy was hurled from a third-story window to land with both legs broken on a street littered with burning beds and other household furniture. . . . Jewish shop windows by the hundreds were systematically and wantonly smashed throughout the entire city. . . . Three synagogues in Leipzig were [torched] simultaneously by incendiary bombs and all sacred objects and records desecrated or destroyed, in most cases hurled through the windows and burned in the streets.

Germans survey the damage to a Jewish-owned storefront after *Kristallnacht*, a Nazi-orchestrated rampage against Jews and Jewish businesses and homes that took place in November 1938.

By the time the fury had played itself out the following day, 96 Jews were dead, and 30,000 had been arrested. More than 1,000 synagogues had been vandalized and burned, Jewish cemeteries had been desecrated, and 7,000 Jewish businesses had been ransacked and destroyed.

It wasn't enough for the Nazis. On November 12, Hermann Göring convened a meeting to discuss measures to purge the German economy of all Jewish influence. The resulting decrees brought financial ruin to German Jews. No Jewish-owned businesses were permitted to reopen after *Kristallnacht* unless they were managed by non-Jews. Jews could no longer work in retail business or be managers or executives of any kind. The laws virtually eliminated the possibility of Jews earning wages at all.

The cost of the damage and destruction wreaked during *Kristallnacht* was staggering—and the Nazis demanded that the Jews, who had been the victims of the attack, bear the financial burden. All insurance payments to Jewish property owners were confiscated. The Jews were declared legally liable for all damages caused during *Kristallnacht,* a total that amounted to 1 billion Reichmarks (about $400 million). "The swine won't commit another murder," Göring was overheard saying, referring to the death of the Paris embassy worker. "Incidentally," he declared ominously, "I would not like to be a Jew in Germany."

By year's end, Hitler and his henchmen were discussing ways to resolve "the Jewish problem" in Germany once and for all. Still on his quest for *Lebensraum*, Hitler was now looking eastward, to Poland, to obtain additional territory. But Poland had the largest Jewish population in Europe—more than 3 million people. So it would be imperative, the Nazis believed, to come up with a viable solution for eliminating the growing Jewish population of the Reich.

A Living Hell

Scene from the Warsaw ghetto, 1942. Walled off from the outside world, residents of the Jewish ghettos faced poverty, hunger, and hopelessness.

"Today almost six million Jews are doomed to be pent up in places where they are not wanted, and for whom the world is divided into places where they cannot live, and places into which they cannot enter."

— Jewish leader Chaim Weizmann, in 1937

The German assault on Jews intensified in 1939. Still, the pressure tactics to force emigration—the countless laws that had stripped them of their rights and left them homeless and destitute, the acts of violence against them—had not been enough to drive a majority of the Jews out of Germany. Adolf Hitler discussed more effective alternatives with Nazi officials. Threatening remaining Jews with severe punishments such as life imprisonment was one option. Escalating forced emigration—rounding up Jews and "dumping" them along the German-Polish border—seemed to be another option. In Hitler's mind, one thing was clear: the Jews had to go.

On January 30, 1939, the Führer publicly announced for the first time his threat to annihilate European Jews. In an address to the Reichstag, he derided Jews for having scorned him when he was attaining power:

> During the time of my struggle for power it was . . . only the Jewish race that received my prophesies with laughter when I said that I would one day take over the leadership of the . . . whole nation, and that I would then among other things settle the Jewish problem. . . . Today I will once more be a prophet: if the international Jewish financiers in and outside Europe should succeed in plunging the nations once more into a world war, then the result will not be . . . the victory of Jewry, but the annihilation of the Jewish race throughout Europe.

Hitler had long made it clear that he believed the Jews were responsible for World War I and for the miseries visited on a defeated Germany. But was he now also revealing his plans to start another war? Certainly it appeared that he was inching closer to war when, on March 15, he defied the terms of the Munich Pact and ordered troops to invade Czechoslovakia. Having seized that country, he also declared the provinces of Bohemia and Moravia to be "protectorates" of the Reich. The number of Jews now trapped in the Third Reich's sphere of influence rose to 750,000.

For Jews in German territory, the opportunity to escape dwindled with each passing day. They had exhausted nearly all avenues to freedom. The United States refused to accept more than its self-imposed quota of 27,000 immigrants annually. Great Britain had issued the British White Paper, a document that severely limited Jewish immigration to Palestine, an area over which the English had administrative control. Argentina, Mexico, Costa Rica, and Brazil had taken in approximately 80,000 Jews, but their resources were rapidly being exhausted.

Throughout the spring and summer of 1939, Hitler prepared for an invasion of Poland, home to more than 3 million of the approximately 6.5 million Jews living in eastern Europe. But the *Führer's* territorial ambitions didn't end with Poland. Ultimately he planned to push further east, into the Soviet Union. An additional 3 million Jews lived in the Soviet Union and the Baltic states of Estonia, Lithuania, and Latvia. If the Nazis moved against these territories, then the millions of Jews living in eastern Europe would be condemned to the same fate as their western counterparts.

At this point, however, Hitler didn't think that Germany was ready for a war with the Soviet Union, which shared a border with Poland. So he forged a treaty with Soviet leader Joseph Stalin, which the two men signed on August 23, 1939. Under the terms of the so-called nonaggression pact, both countries agreed to remain neutral and to refrain from acts of aggression against each other if either went to war with another country. A secret clause in the pact also allowed for the partition of Poland: Hitler would acquire western and central Poland, Stalin the eastern third. The Soviets would also be permitted to carve up the Baltic states without German interference.

With Hitler's defiance of the terms of the Munich Pact, Great Britain and France realized that he was not to be trusted and began gearing up for war. They had also offered guarantees to other potential victims of German

(continued on p. 80)

THE VOYAGE OF THE *ST. LOUIS*

After the dismal failure of the Evian Conference, European Jews desperately sought ways to flee Nazi-occupied territories. Traveling by land across Europe's political borders was nearly impossible, so some Jews tried to leave the continent altogether. Yet this prospect was extremely difficult as well: refugees had to secure an available ship and willing crew and raise enough money to buy

The St. Louis *in the port of Havana, Cuba.*

passage on the vessel. Even then, they had no guarantee that the ship would actually sail—or that it would reach a friendly harbor. The plight of one group of Jews attempting to take a ship to safety—those who traveled on the *St. Louis*—captured international media attention.

On May 13, 1939, the *St. Louis* sailed from Hamburg, Germany, bound for Havana, Cuba, with 937 passengers aboard. Most were Jews fleeing Nazi oppression. The passengers believed that they had purchased legitimate landing certificates from Manuel Benitez Gonzales, the director-general of Cuba's immigration office, and expected to be permitted temporary sanctuary in Cuba until they received U.S. visas. What they didn't know, however, was that eight days before the *St. Louis* sailed, Cuban president Federico Laredo Bru had invalidated all landing certificates issued by Benitez Gonzales. A large anti-Semitic demonstration had taken place in Havana before the *St. Louis* even left Hamburg. In Cuba's depressed economy, native Cubans feared and resented new immigrants, who they believed would take jobs away from them.

When the *St. Louis* arrived at Havana on May 27, only 28 passengers with valid documents were permitted to disembark. Lawrence Berenson, a lawyer who represented the American Joint Distribution Committee (JDC), attempted to negotiate an agreement with President Bru to allow the remaining immigrants into Cuba. Bru refused, ordering the *St. Louis* to leave Cuban waters.

In the hope that the United States would allow its passengers direct entry, the *St. Louis* sailed toward Miami. But America also refused to accept the refugees, citing immigration quota restrictions.

The *St. Louis* had no choice but to return to Europe. While it was en route, England, France, Belgium, and the Netherlands agreed to take in its passengers, and after a 35-day return voyage, the *St. Louis* docked at Antwerp, Belgium.

Of the 937 passengers given asylum, only the 287 whom England accepted remained safe from Nazi extermination. Less than three months after the ship reached land, Hitler invaded Poland and ignited World War II. Those who had taken refuge in France, Belgium, and the Netherlands were eventually taken to labor or death camps, where it is believed they all died.

(continued from p. 77)

aggression, including Poland. On September 1, German troops launched a full-scale invasion of Poland, and just two days later, Great Britain and France declared war on Germany. In keeping with the nonaggression pact, the Soviet Union invaded western Poland two weeks later, on September 17. Soviet troops met little resistance, since Polish forces were still struggling to stave off the overwhelming German onslaught.

Germany was employing a military tactic the Nazi High Command termed a *blitzkrieg* ("lightning war"). "By using swiftly moving [military] spearheads, assault teams of infantry, and a system of air-to-ground coordination of fighter planes, the Nazis engaged in a lightning war involving one million infantry, 1,500 fighter planes, and about 1,000 tanks," relates Dan Cohn-Sherbok in *Understanding the Holocaust*. Overwhelmed by the dual assaults from Germany and the Soviet Union, Poland's capital city of Warsaw fell within the month.

Following closely on the heels of German front-line troops were the *Einsatzgruppen*—the German SS Special Action Group, commonly referred to as mobile killing squads. They plundered Jewish communities in Poland, confiscating property and personal possessions before rounding up Jews for confinement. They seemed to enjoy random murders and the looting, desecration, and burning of synagogues. They delighted in inflicting pain and humiliating their terrified captives. Jewish properties were set ablaze with people inside; anyone who tried to escape the infernos was shot. In the village of Piotrkow, religious Jews were forced to scrub toilets with their prayer shawls. In Raciaz, religious Jewish men were ushered into the streets, where their beards and sidelocks were cut off. Such atrocities and humiliations were repeated in hundreds of Jewish towns and villages throughout Poland.

Upon its surrender, Poland disappeared as a European country. Germany and the Soviet Union divided the conquered territory as they had agreed, Germany acquiring western and central Poland, and the Soviets gaining the eastern third of the country along with the promise of seizing Estonia, Lithuania, Latvia, and Finland without German interference. Hitler divided his new territory into districts. Districts in western Poland were incorporated into the Reich as *Lebensraum* for Germans. Those in central Poland, which included Lodz, Krakow, Lublin, Radom, Lvov, Kielce, and Warsaw, fell under the General Government—the region with the highest concentration of Jews.

As the German military secured the Reich's new territory, Hitler's High Command met in Berlin to discuss what to do with the millions of Polish Jews now under German rule. Reinhard Heydrich identified two

An SS soldier humiliates an Orthodox Polish Jew by publicly trimming his beard. Germany's invasion of Poland on September 1, 1939, triggered World War II— and eventually brought 3 million more Jews under Nazi control.

immediate remedies. First, he proposed that all Jews be removed from the western districts. Second, since cities such as Warsaw already had large Jewish populations, he recommended "relocating" Jews from outlying villages into the urban areas of the General Government. Essentially, the entire Jewish population of central and western Poland would be concentrated within the cities of central Poland.

Heydrich drafted a memo outlining the procedures for completing this relocation to "Jewish residential quarters." The first step in "the final aim," Heydrich wrote, "is the concentration of the Jews from the countryside into the larger cities." Specifically, the concentration centers needed to be near railway lines or at rail junctions, which would ease the burden of transporting large numbers of people at once. It was imperative, Heydrich said, that the deportations be completed quickly. The job of executing Heydrich's directive fell to the chiefs of the *Einsatzgruppen*.

Realizing that the Jewish residential quarters required a set of regulations for day-to-day management, Heydrich further ordered that each Jewish district establish and maintain a *Judenrat,* a council of Jewish elders composed of local rabbis and other highly respected community members. Each *Judenrat* would be responsible for implementing orders issued by the Reich. It was this memo, released on September 21, 1939, that created the horrific Jewish ghettos of Poland.

Before the ghettos were ready to accept transports, Jews were shuttled to isolated, undeveloped areas far from large settlements. On October 17, 1939, for example, about 1,200 Czechoslovakian Jews were rounded up from Moravska Ostrava and crowded into waiting railway cars, not knowing where they were going or what their fate would be when they arrived at their destination. After a long, harsh journey without food or water, the

WOHNGEBIET DER
JUDEN
BETRETEN
VERBOTEN

Jews in the train cars stopped in Zarzecze, Poland. SS official Adolf Eichmann was there to greet them. "About seven or eight kilometers from here, across the river San, the *Führer* of the Jews has promised you a new homeland," Eichmann said. "There are no apartments and no houses—if you will build your homes you will have a roof over your head." The plan was to create a forced-labor camp, a kind of Jewish reservation in Poland. This idea was later abandoned, however.

Once relocation centers had been put in place, Germany began deporting Austrian and Czech Jews to the General Government district of Poland. The resettlement was a massive undertaking. Tens of thousands of Jews were

Pedestrians cross the street dividing the two parts of the Lodz ghetto, where 164,000 Jews were forced to live in an area of only 1.5 square miles. The sign says, "Jewish residential area. Entrance is forbidden."

forcibly removed from their homes, often with little or no notice, permitted to take only the possessions they could carry on their backs or load into a small cart. Many who lived in rural areas were simply loaded on trucks themselves and transported to the nearest rail station for deportation to the ghettos.

The first Polish ghetto was established in early November 1939 in Piotrovkov Trybunalski, a village of 69,000 Polish Jews near the city of Lodz. The following spring, the Lodz ghetto itself was established. One hundred sixty-four thousand Jews were forced to live in 1.5 square miles of space—a population seven times greater than before the German occupation.

With astounding speed and efficiency, the Nazis established several more ghettos: Warsaw (1940), the largest ghetto, where almost half a million people were forced to live; Krakow (March 1941); Lublin and Radom (April 1941); and Lvov (December 1941). By the end of that year, the relocation was complete. Virtually all of Poland's Jews had been packed into run-down, overcrowded settlements in the General Government district. Thousands of Jews from other territories of the Reich, such as western Poland, Bohemia, and Austria, arrived on foot, by truck, or by railcar to be imprisoned behind the cement-block walls and barbed-wire fences of Jewish ghettos.

The ghettos were a living hell. Once a ghetto had been closed in, it became a crime punishable by death for a Jew to step beyond its walls. Living conditions were deplorable: apartment spaces intended for 4 people were occupied by 10 or 15. Many had no rooms at all and took refuge in stairwells or hallways. Starvation was a constant threat, since people typically subsisted on around 1,100 calories a day (about one-fourth of a normal day's food intake). The water supply was contaminated, the plumbing dilapidated, and sanitation woefully inadequate.

A young girl holds her little sister, who is either unconscious or dead, in the Warsaw ghetto. Starvation and disease claimed the lives of thousands of Jews in the ghettos—but the death rate wasn't high enough to suit the Nazis.

Tuberculosis and typhoid raged through the settlements. In the winter it was nearly impossible to stay warm.

The Reich had ordered compulsory labor for ghetto Jews aged 14 to 60. This slave labor was of great benefit in Germany's war effort. Early concentration camps had been constructed to house enemies of the state and other prisoners, and now, with the creation of ghettos, dozens more camps sprang up throughout Nazi-controlled Europe. Thousands of men, women, and teens were transported daily from the ghettos to various labor camps, where they made clothes, shoes, and ammunition or were forced to haul tar, rocks, and concrete to repair war-damaged roads and buildings.

Milton Meltzer, the author of *Never to Forget,* describes in his book the forced-labor experiences of Holocaust survivor Reuben Rosenberg, who lived in the Lublin ghetto. Reuben was 11 years old when World War II began in 1939; after working at labor camps in Deblin and Czestochowa, he was transported to Flossenbürg, where prisoners were put to work in a granite quarry, armaments factories, and aircraft factories. More than 65,000 prisoners passed through the Flossenbürg camp's gates between 1938 and 1945. Rosenberg describes his life there:

> At this camp there was a factory that made bazookas. There was one SS man for every four prisoners. Every day 15 men died, aside from those who died from "natural causes." We ran to work. Work intended for 20 people was done by ten. We worked from 6 A.M. to 7 P.M. We collapsed. Many people committed suicide. In two weeks, 500 died. Filth, no water, two days without heat, no bath, and no underwear. There were 25 lashes for stealing potato peelings. They called us the race gang, communists, cadets, soapbags, criminals, and Bolsheviks. . . .
>
> Because things were bad at the front, they hurried us and always beat us at the factory. . . . To load bazookas we had to use [toxic] picric acid and trotil. We worked without gas masks, and after a few weeks the lungs and feet would cave in. The young were chosen for this task. SS men would kill them while they worked, so there was always a shortage of workers.

Many German industrial companies, including I.G. Farben, Junger, and Krupp, took advantage of the slave labor from the ghettos. The workers never received wages; the money they would have earned went directly to the SS and into Reich accounts. Prisoners were forced to work 10- to 12-hour days with little food and almost no breaks. All of this suited the Nazis well: after all, working the Jews to death or starving them certainly helped

reduce their numbers. They died by the hundreds—in the streets, in stairwells and hallways, on sidewalks propped up against buildings. Corpses became so commonplace in Jewish ghettos that after a while, those who were still alive barely noticed the pervasiveness of death.

But this "natural reduction" process was slow, and the Reich didn't have years to wait. As Hitler's armies marched into Denmark, Norway, the Netherlands, Belgium, Luxembourg, and France in 1940, and into Yugoslavia and Greece in 1941, it seemed that all of Europe was within his grasp. He turned his attention once more to the east. The nonaggression pact of 1939 now meant nothing to him; he intended to invade the Soviet Union. First, however, he needed to determine the fate of the millions of Jews now living in German territories. A "Final Solution" to the Jewish problem was at hand.

Dachau concentration camp prisoners assemble shells for the German war effort. The Nazis frequently worked camp inmates to death, which not only enabled the production of vast amounts of materiel at low cost but also, the Reich's leaders believed, helped resolve "the Jewish problem."

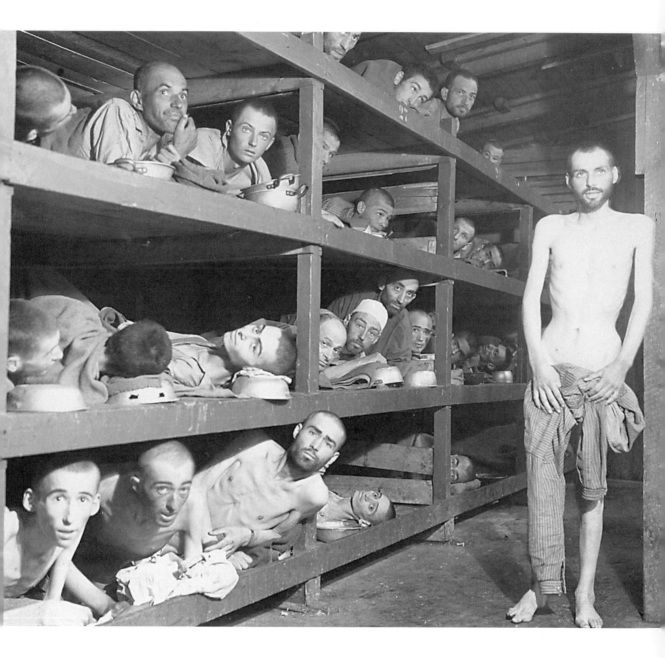

Emaciated prisoners in their barracks at the Buchenwald concentration camp. Conditions in the concentration and extermination camps were so horrifying that their power to appall hasn't diminished even after more than half a century.

The Most Terrible Place on Earth

One of only a tenth of a transport of Jews to survive the initial sorting, [a witness at Auschwitz] looked about on the evening of his arrival for his companion. A veteran inmate asked him, "Was he sent to the left side?" "Yes," [the witness] replied. "Then you can see him there," [he] was told. "Where?" A hand pointed to the chimney a few hundred yards off, which was sending a column of flame up into the grey sky of Poland.

—Stewart Justman, *The Jewish Holocaust for Beginners*

While Germany attacked Poland in September 1939, Hitler had instituted another kind of assault at home: a program permitting "mercy killings." The euthanasia program, named T-4 after its Berlin office address (Tiergartenstrasse 4), was designed to eliminate the mentally ill, the physically handicapped, the deformed, the incurably

--denn Gott kann nicht wollen, daß Kranke und Sieche sich in Kranken und Siechen fortpflanzen

A frame from a Reich Propaganda Office film-strip promoting the Nazis' program of euthanizing the mentally retarded and physically infirm, because, as the caption states, "God cannot want the sick and ailing to reproduce."

ill—anyone whose physical or mental condition might "contaminate" the purity of the Aryan race.

T-4 was headed by one of Hitler's personal physicians, Karl Brandt. With the cooperation of doctors, nurses, hospital aides, and psychiatric and medical hospital administrators, the program was shockingly successful. Hospital and institutional personnel throughout Germany completed forms that identified their patients' state of health. These forms were then reviewed by experts, who determined the fate of each patient. Their small pencil marks told the chilling tale: a red plus sign next to a name meant death; a blue minus sign meant life. Those marked for extermination were transported to killing centers in Germany and Austria.

Initially, doomed patients were put to death by lethal injection, but in 1940 this method was replaced with poisoning by carbon monoxide. The gassing facilities were disguised as public showers so victims would not panic. In a grisly conclusion to the exterminations, gold fillings in victims' teeth were removed before their corpses were transferred to a crematorium. Nazi officials then prepared false death certificates, placed the ashes of the dead in urns, and issued letters of condolence to the families of the dead. Angry protests mounted over the T-4 program and it was shut down—but not before 70,000 to 300,00 German citizens had been put to death.

After Germany invaded the Soviet Union on June 22, 1941, Soviet Jews and those living in Soviet-occupied territories—a total of 4 million people—were within the murderous reach of the Nazis. No longer did Hitler believe in simply rounding up and confining Jews to ghettos. The success of T-4 convinced him that he could revive the program on a much grander scale as a solution to the Jewish problem. The plan would ultimately result in the vast "killing factories"—the death camps of Auschwitz-Birkenau, Belzec, Chelmno, Madjanek, Sobibor, and Treblinka.

In the meantime, the responsibility for carrying out the killings fell to members of the *Einsatzgruppen*. When Germany invaded Poland, these killing squads had followed the regular troops to execute so-called political enemies and to round up Jews for transport to the ghettos. Now, after the invasion of the Soviet Union, their directive was clearer and more forceful: kill every Jew you encounter in the conquered territories. Only after this initial "cleansing" were remaining Jews to be confined to ghettos.

Battalion-sized units of *Einsatzgruppen* fanned out from occupied Poland, cutting a bloody swath through Jewish towns and villages. In two years, the *Einsatzgruppen* annihilated entire Jewish communities in towns like Kovno, Lithuania; Riga, Latvia; Vilna, Poland; Tallinn, Estonia; and Minsk, in formerly Russian-occupied eastern Poland. They also murdered thousands of non-Jews who opposed the Nazi regime or were considered "contaminants" of the Aryan race: political dissidents, partisans, homosexuals, and Gypsies. The slaughter was often facilitated by local police and other collaborators. The *Einsatzgruppen* C battalion committed one of the largest concentrated mass murders at Babi Yar, Kiev, where 34,000 Jews were shot to death in a two-day killing spree.

At the start of the onslaught, the *Einsatzgruppen*'s weapon of choice was the gun. Typically, a killing squad would enter a village, round up Jewish inhabitants, and march them at gunpoint to a forest or field on the outskirts of the town. There they were forced to disrobe, and then they were shot. After the war, during the trials of Nazi war criminals, a German civil engineer named Hermann Graebe testified to having seen the liquidation of a Jewish ghetto in Dubno, Ukraine:

> The people who had got off the lorries [wagons]—men, women and children of all ages—had to undress upon the order of an SS man who was carrying a riding or dog whip in his hand. They had to place their clothing on separate piles for shoes, clothing, and underwear. I saw a pile of shoes containing approximately 800 to 1,000 pairs, and great heaps of underwear and clothing. Without weeping or crying out these people undressed and stood together in family groups, embracing each other and saying goodbye while waiting for a sign from another SS man, who stood on the edge of the ditch and also had a whip. During the quarter of an hour in which I stood near the ditch, I did not hear a single complaint or plea for mercy. . . .
>
> I walked around the mound and stood in front of the huge grave. . . . I turned my eyes towards the man doing the shooting. He was an SS man; he sat, legs swinging, on the edge of the ditch. He had an automatic rifle resting

As the German armies rolled through eastern Europe, *Einsatzgruppen*—mobile killing squads—followed in the wake of the front-line units. Their mission: to exterminate Jews in the newly conquered territory. Here an *Einsatzgruppe* member prepares to shoot a Ukrainian Jew.

on his knees. . . . The [victims], completely naked, climbed down steps which had been cut into the clay wall of the ditch, stumbled over the heads of those lying there [already dead] and stopped at the spot indicated by the SS man. . . . Then I heard a series of rifle shots.

In all, approximately 1.2 million Jews—roughly one-quarter of all those who died in the Holocaust—were murdered by *Einsatzgruppen* squads.

But the shootings were an inefficient way to kill large groups of people, and the massacres began to wear on some *Einsatzgruppen* members. Many began to drink heavily; others justified their work by using euphemistic terms like "cleansing" or "liquidation" to describe what they were doing. Words like "murder," "massacre," and "killing" were never uttered.

The Nazis had been experimenting with other killing methods, including the method used in the T-4 program. They developed mobile killing units—hermetically sealed vans into which carbon monoxide was pumped. The vans held 90 people at a time, and these executions could be completed in less than 15 minutes. Moreover, the *Einsatzgruppen* no longer needed to witness victims dying. After the gassings, the vans were driven to a designated site, where the bodies were removed by Jewish prisoners and dumped into mass graves. When the Nazis opened the first extermination camp at Chelmno, Poland, in December 1941, these vans were used to kill the Jews transported from the Lodz ghetto.

In just eight years, European Jews had endured anti-Semitic campaigns, vandalism, anti-Jewish propaganda, and wave upon wave of legislated persecution. They were forced to wear Star of David patches on their outer garments and carry passports marked with red *J*s to identify them as Jews. After Germany invaded Poland, their homes, businesses, and possessions were confiscated. They were herded like cattle into locked, walled ghettos, sealed off from the world, unable to work and barely subsisting. They were forced into slave labor camps, and when that did not kill them quickly enough, they were shot and gassed to death, their bodies dumped in mass graves. From prejudice to persecution to mass murder—but still, it was not enough to satisfy the Nazis. Nothing short of total annihilation was acceptable.

At the end of July 1941, Hermann Göring ordered Reinhard Heydrich to develop a comprehensive plan for settling the so-called Jewish problem. Before the year ended, an unthinkable blueprint had been developed. Under the code name *Aktion Reinhard*, the Nazis began constructing three camps—Belzec, Sobibor, and Treblinka II. Their express function was to accelerate the extermination of Jews.

Six months later, on January 20, 1942, Heydrich assembled a group of high-ranking government and military officials in the affluent Berlin suburb of Wannsee. The primary purpose of the conference was to unveil the official Final Solution to the Jewish problem. The conference was not intended to be a forum for debate; rather, it was a discussion of how best to implement the already accepted plan.

The extermination of European Jews had reached its third and most monstrous stage: the murder of thousands of Jews each day in huge gassing chambers—a vastly more "efficient" way to commit genocide. The process was gruesomely systematic. Eventually the populations of the ghettos would be liquidated, transported by railcar to the six death camps in Poland. Those few who arrived at these camps still fit for hard labor were directed to their right. The rest were sent to the left, supposedly for delousing in public showers—but in reality for extermination in the gas chambers.

Although Adolf Eichmann and his SS staff conducted the liquidation, the actual relocation and extermination required the work of thousands. The Polish railway system provided the crucial link. All six death camps were situated along rail lines, and 1.4 million workers of the *Reichsbahn* (Germany's railroad system) handled the logistics of acquiring freight cars, coordinating schedules, keeping rail lines in operation, and conducting the trains.

Jews assemble in the street for the liquidation of their eastern European ghetto. Unbeknownst to the men, women, and children in this photo, their destination is a death camp.

In the meantime, trains carrying supplies for German soldiers on two fronts had to be kept running regularly as well. Other participants were also necessary. As Michael Berenbaum relates in *The World Must Know*:

> Parish churches and the Interior Ministry supplied the birth records that defined and isolated Jews. The Post Office delivered the notifications of definition, expropriation, denaturalization, and deportation. The Finance Ministry confiscated Jewish wealth and property; German industrial and commercial firms fired Jewish workers, officers, and board members, even disenfranchising Jewish stockholders. . . . Government transportation bureaus handled billing arrangements with the railroads for the trains that carried Jews to their death.

The first Jews deported to the death camps were those in the Lodz ghetto, resettled there from Germany, Austria, Luxembourg, Bohemia, and Moravia. The

Judenrat of the ghettos were often forced by the Nazis to choose which residents would be transported—but the Nazis themselves concealed the true fate of the transportees, telling them that they were being resettled again. It didn't take long, however, for rumors of the death camps to filter into the Jewish ghettos.

Before the deportations began, the *Judenrat* had the unenviable responsibility of satisfying both the directives of their Nazi captors and the needs of the young, old, infirm, and overworked citizens in their charge. Some, like Lodz ghetto chairman Mordechai Chaim Rumkowski, tried to make their communities indispensable by maintaining a pool of strong and healthy workers for the Nazi slave forces. Once liquidations began, however, *Judenrat* members had no choice but to comply with the Nazis. If they did not, Nazi soldiers simply swept through the ghettos and removed people by force.

In the first six months of 1942, more than 60,000 Jews and Gypsies were deported from the Lodz ghetto and gassed at Chelmno. In the summer of 1942, approximately 300,000 Jews from the Warsaw ghetto were taken to their deaths at Treblinka. Children were not spared or sheltered from the horrors of the Final Solution: more than 1.5 million of them died in the Holocaust. Warsaw *Judenrat* chairman Adam Czerniaków attempted to save the children and orphans under his charge, but he was unsuccessful. Among those liquidated during that horrible season were famed Polish educator-doctor Janusz Korczak and the 192 children in his orphanage.

Between 1941 and 1944, railcars filled almost beyond capacity with deported Jews rolled continually along the tracks of Europe to the death camps. In many cases the condemned endured several such trips. For example, the Jews in western Europe who were being deported to the east were sent to transit camps like Westerbork,

Polish doctor Janusz Korczak with some of the Jewish children from his orphanage. Though he had many opportunities to escape the Nazis, Korczak refused to abandon the orphans. In August 1942 he and all 192 of his young charges were deported to Treblinka, where they were put to death.

in the Netherlands, or Theresienstadt, in Czechoslovakia, before being reboarded on another train that took them to the eastern ghettos. From there, they were once more crammed into railcars for their final journey.

The journey to a death camp often took days, even a full week. The crushing weight of human cargo slowed the trains to speeds of just 25 to 30 miles per hour. Very little food or water was provided, and sanitary conditions were appalling. Constructed for cattle or freight, the railcars were poorly ventilated and often arrived at the camps with hundreds of Jews already dead inside, either from suffocating heat and lack of air during summer months or from freezing temperatures during winters.

Even deportees who had heard the rumors about killing centers quietly—and desperately—hoped they weren't true. Those who survived these journeys arrived at the camps feeling grateful to be alive and believing that they had endured the worst. Frightened, exhausted, and weak from their journey, they offered little resistance when Nazi soldiers opened the railcar doors and rousted them out onto train platforms.

The largest and by far the most infamous death camp was Auschwitz-Birkenau, near Kraków, Poland. Auschwitz was actually a vast complex that included a "concentration" center for criminal prisoners and forced-labor workers, and an extermination system consisting of four huge gas chambers. More people were slaughtered at Auschwitz than at any other camp. Today the very name still carries a chilling resonance. A survivor of the notorious camp, "Edith P.," struggles to find words for its horrors in Joshua M. Greene and Shiva Kumar's book, *Witness: Voices from the Holocaust:*

> Auschwitz, if I would like to describe it, I would say there is—there has not—there has not been—people—people did not invent an expression [for] what Auschwitz was. It was hell on earth. And the silence of Auschwitz was hell. The nights were hell. And the days—somehow we—we got up at three o'clock in the morning, and at four o'clock summertime or four-thirty, when the sun came up, it was not like the sun—I swear to you! It was not bright. It was always red to me; it was always black to me. . . . The sun was never beautiful. And when the moon was out, it [also] meant only destruction. We almost forgot what life was all about. And in the evening, when you dared to go out and you saw the flames of the crematorium. . . . [There was] the smell of the human flesh, which we didn't know it was. We were young kids, inexperienced of such horror. Who is experienced in such ways?

Adding to the nightmare were the ghoulish "medical experiments" conducted on inmates of Auschwitz by SS doctors. They included forced sterilization and altitude and hypothermia tests. The most nefarious Nazi physician, Josef Mengele, conducted painful and brutal tests on dwarfs, Gypsies, and twins in the name of medical research, and he used the results of the Auschwitz experiments to bolster Nazi claims about the superiority of the Aryan race.

Jews who arrived at Auschwitz still able to walk were separated by gender and lined up for an initial *selektion*. An SS officer then performed on-the-spot assessments—a nod to the right meant you would be tattooed with a number, de-loused, and used for slave labor; a nod to the left meant you were destined for one of the gas chambers. There you relinquished your remaining valuables, undressed completely, and entered the chamber, where you were asphyxiated with thousands of others.

Efficiency of killing was the primary objective in the death camps, so when Auschwitz commandant Rudolf Höss was ordered to prepare the camp for large-scale exterminations, he searched for a more lethal alternative to carbon monoxide poisoning. A highly poisonous cyanic gas called Zyklon B (hydrogen cyanide), normally used for fumigation, had been tested on a group of Soviet prisoners of war and proved more than satisfactory for the death chambers: it killed victims in large numbers in less than 15 minutes. It was employed exclusively at Auschwitz at first, and then later at Majdanek. Zyklon B was manufactured as crystal pellets, which were sealed in tin canisters. Once exposed to the air, the crystals vaporized into the deadly gas that asphyxiated its victims almost instantly.

After the victims were packed into the gas chambers, the steel doors were sealed shut and the lights extinguished. Those who were assigned "death duty" then dropped Zyklon B pellets into a vent in the ceiling that led

to the chamber floor. As the pellets vaporized, the ago-
nized victims suffocated. When all were dead, huge
exhaust fans were turned on in the chamber to clear the
air before the bodies were removed and the next group
was crammed inside.

Sonderkommandos—Jewish forced-labor prisoners
assigned to the killing chambers—then removed the
corpses and placed them on elevators to be taken to the
crematoria. Before they placed the bodies in the furnaces,
however, the *Sonderkommandos* were required to shave
the hair from the heads of the corpses and extract gold
fillings from the victims' teeth. The gold was melted

Jews arriving at Auschwitz-
Birkenau go through the
selection process. Those
deemed strong enough to
work are sent to the right.
All others are sent to the
left, to be gassed.

down and formed into bars for the Reich's war chest; the human hair was shipped to Germany, where it was used to stuff mattresses and make socks for German submarine crews. The ashes from the furnaces were removed and used as fertilizer. Even in death, the Jews and other victims of Nazi atrocities were still being stripped of all that was theirs.

For those who did not perish in the gas chambers, life at Auschwitz and the other camps was unbearable. Inmates, barely fed enough food to survive until their next meal, were subjected to random beatings and forced to stand for hours at a time during roll calls. Stables built to hold 48 horses were converted to barracks housing 800 prisoners. Packed together on bunks made of wooden planks, inmates slept six to a row with meager covers and no padding, pillows, or heat. A single bucket served for a toilet. The bunks were so narrow that when one person turned, his or her bunkmates also had to turn. Even in sleep, they could not escape misery.

Each day, inmates watched the seemingly endless arrival of trains, filled with people who they knew would be dead within hours. At the height of the killings, the gas chambers and crematoria operated around the clock. Laborers could see black smoke plumes drifting from towering chimneys, each puff all that remained of a mother or father, a wife or husband, a child. The acrid smell of burnt human flesh hung constantly in the air.

Most of those who were not immediately exterminated wasted away from starvation or disease. Weak, exhausted, and dehydrated, they shuffled about like human phantoms. The camp yards were littered with prisoners who simply dropped dead where they stood. The emaciated corpses were piled like cords of wood outside barracks, along roads, or wherever else there was room. Inmates who fought to survive faced life in the

most terrible place on earth—a place designed to strip them of all dignity, all hope, and all humanity before extinguishing their existence.

The Jews who arrived at the gates of the death camps had lived and worked in every corner of Europe. They came from Austria, Belgium, Czechoslovakia, France, Greece, Italy, Lithuania, Norway, Poland, and Yugoslavia. When the massacres finally ceased, more than 150,000 Jews had perished at Chelmno, 600,000 at Belzec, and 360,000 at Majdanek. A quarter million had died at Sobibor, 870,000 at Treblinka. And at Auschwitz-Birkenau, 1.1 million Jews had been exterminated.

The Auschwitz prisoners at the left of this photo are completing construction of the ovens at the Birkenau crematoria. Soon the crematoria would be operating 24 hours a day burning the bodies of murdered Jews.

"Remember
. . . Never
Forget"

*"It was a period in history when civilization lost its humanity and humanity lost
its soul."*

—Elie Wiesel, Nobel laureate and Holocaust survivor

Though the extermination of the Jews continued unabated through 1944, the tide of war had long since turned against Germany. On December 7, 1941, Germany's ally Japan had launched a surprise attack on the U.S. Pacific Fleet at Pearl Harbor, Hawaii, drawing America into the war. The addition of millions of American fighting men, along with the massive industrial output of the U.S. economy, helped tip the scales in favor of the Allies.

In addition, despite quick victories during the early part of the campaign, Hitler's invasion of the Soviet Union turned out to be a huge tactical mistake. By December 1941, the German offensive had stalled within 25 miles of the Soviet capital, Moscow. Believing that a swift victory was attainable, Hitler and his military leaders had made no provisions for cold-weather fighting. With the onset of the bitter Russian winter—and facing a fierce Soviet counter-offensive—the Wehrmacht, Germany's army, suddenly found itself in desperate straits. German soldiers lacked warm clothing, their equipment froze, and food and fuel supplies were quickly depleted. The goal of quickly knocking out the Soviet Union had to be abandoned, and Germany was now committed to fighting a war on two fronts.

As the Soviet Red Army ground down the Wehrmacht on the eastern front, the other Allies—Great Britain, the United States, and, to a lesser extent, Free France—pressed the Nazis on the western front. Invasions of North Africa, Sicily, Italy, and especially the June 1944 D-day invasion of Normandy shrank Nazi-controlled territory. By the summer of 1944, many of Hitler's highest officials began to realize that the war was lost. For the first time, they began to talk of surrender. That year, an attempt to assassinate the *Führer* with a bomb was carried out at a Nazi conference, though Hitler was only slightly injured. Verging on insanity—and now completely distrustful of his own military officials—Hitler sequestered himself in an underground bunker in Berlin, where he continued to direct the war.

Despite the reversal of Germany's fortunes on the battlefield, the Nazis continued to transport Jews and other "undesirables" to the death camps. By now, the extermination efforts were getting in the way of supplying the armies at the fronts. In spite of the pleas of several of his officers to divert resources from the death camps into the failing war effort, Hitler refused even to discuss the possibility. To the end, one of his most important goals was to ensure the complete annihilation of European Jewry. "Above all," he wrote in a political statement just one day before his death, "I enjoin the government and the people to uphold the race laws to limit and to resist mercilessly the poisoner of all nations, international Jewry." On April 30, 1945, Hitler committed suicide by shooting himself in his Berlin bunker. Eight days later, Germany surrendered.

The enormity of the Nazi extermination program would become apparent only after Allied troops entered Germany. Witnesses were enraged and repelled by the Germans' appalling brutality, but many also wondered about the Jews' apparent submissiveness to their captors. In the film *Genocide*, which recounts the horrors of the Holocaust, the narrator begins by addressing that very question:

> People often ask, "Why did the Jews go like sheep to the slaughter?" Sheep to the slaughter? How can they know what it was like, crowded together in a way that even animals are not treated—weakened by months of hardship and hunger, locked up in sealed wagons, without food, weapons, without friends, knowing that if even one escaped the Nazis, who was there that would welcome them, who cared? Who would lift a finger? . . . Sheep to the slaughter? What do those who use the phrase know about honor, about the thousands of parents who would not desert their little ones, who stayed behind to embrace them, cuddle them, to exchange glances with them just one more time? What do they know about reverence, about those who gave up their daily ration of food so that a father, a grandmother, a rabbi might live another day? What do they know of a people who refused to believe in the death of mankind, who in forsaken places called hell organized schools, prayed and studied Talmud, wrote poems, composed lyrics, sang songs of today, of eternity, of tomorrow, even when there was to be no tomorrow?

In fact, Jews did perform many acts of resistance against the Nazis, some of them impulsive and others carefully organized. The latter took many forms, and underground resistance groups often used smuggled weapons to attack their persecutors. In each case, they believed that even the smallest act of revolt made a powerful statement, if not to the Nazis then to other Jews who felt helpless to stop the madness of the Holocaust.

Perhaps the most significant armed revolt of Jews against the Nazi regime was the Warsaw ghetto uprising, which began on April 19, 1943. After ghetto residents learned that approximately 300,000 Jews deported from there had been massacred at Treblinka, a group of survivors still living in the ghetto decided to resist. They formed an organization known as Z.O.B. (from the Polish *Zydowska Organizacja Bojowa,* or "Jewish Fighting Organization"). Led by Mordecai Anielewicz, they prepared to fight when the Nazis came to round them up and load them on cattle cars for deportation to a death camp.

The Z.O.B. issued a proclamation to Warsaw ghetto residents: "Jewish masses," it declared, "the hour is drawing near. You must be prepared to resist. Not a single Jew should go to the railroad cars. Those who are unable to put up active resistance should resist passively, should go into hiding. . . . Our slogan must be: All are ready to die as human beings."

The Germans had planned to liquidate the ghetto's remaining 55,000 Jews over a three-day period, but through courageous organized resistance, the Jews held the Germans at bay for an entire month. Severely outnumbered and armed with few weapons—after the uprising the Germans recovered less than a dozen rifles, 59 handguns, and a few hundred grenades and other explosives— the resistance fighters engaged in full-scale combat with the Germans and forced them to retreat not once but twice.

Scattered fighting continued for days afterward. Finally, the Nazis issued an order to burn the ghetto to the ground. Despite its outcome, the Warsaw ghetto uprising remains a symbolic victory. The revolt sent a powerful message to Nazi persecutors—that Europe's Jews were willing to die fighting.

Even in the death camps themselves, facing staggering odds, some Jews rebelled against their captors. In May 1943 at Treblinka, 1,000 prisoners armed with shovels and a few firearms revolted and set fire to part of the camp. About 200 prisoners escaped. At Auschwitz-Birkenau too, the *Sonderkommandos* blew up one of the four crematoria with dynamite they had smuggled out of a munitions factory where some were forced to work. About 600 prisoners managed to escape in the wake of the explosion.

As the Allied troops closed in on Germany, the Nazis began frantically destroying evidence of their murderous atrocities. Gas chambers and crematoria were demolished.

With thick smoke in the background a testament to the ferocity of the fighting, German soldiers march away Jews captured during the Warsaw ghetto uprising. For 20 days in April and May of 1943, the lightly armed residents of the ghetto held 1,200 SS, Wehrmacht, and police troops at bay.

Camps were cleared of remaining inmates, who were sent on brutal forced marches in the dead of winter to labor camps deeper within Germany. Hundreds died on these marches—some lasting up to a month—from starvation, exhaustion, and exposure. Prisoners who faltered along the way were simply shot or left for dead.

When Allied troops penetrated German-occupied territories, they came upon hundreds of labor camps that the retreating Nazis had simply abandoned. For the prisoners left behind, the experience was eerie. They would awake one morning to realize that something unusual had happened: there had been no roll call to rouse them from sleep. A few would bravely step outside their barracks to survey the camp, only to discover that the SS guards were gone and the camp grounds deserted.

The Soviets were the first to liberate one of the Nazi camps. On July 23, 1944, they came upon the death camp of Majdanek, just outside Lublin, Poland. They were ill-prepared for the horror they encountered. In a report filed less than a month later, Soviet correspondent Roman Karman described the ghastly scene:

> I have never seen a more abominable sight than Majdanek near Lublin, Hitler's notorious *Vernichtungslager,* where more than half a million European men, women, and children were massacred. . . . This is not a concentration camp; it is a gigantic murder plant. . . .
>
> In the center of the camp stands a huge stone building with a factory chimney—the world's biggest crematorium. . . . The gas chambers contained some 250 people at a time. They were [so] closely packed . . . that after [the victims] suffocated they remained standing. . . . It is difficult to believe it myself, but human eyes cannot deceive me.

The Soviets also came upon the Belzec, Sobibor, and Treblinka death camps. Though the Germans had already "liquidated" the prisoners and had attempted to camouflage their atrocities, Soviet soldiers encountered unspeakably gruesome sights, stumbling across human bones sticking out of the ground from mass graves where the Nazis had dumped their victims. The reports that filtered out of Germany from Soviet, British, and American troops were so horrific that many people simply could not comprehend them.

The Soviets initially refrained from releasing any reports about what they found on January 27, 1945, at Auschwitz-Birkenau. Walking skeletons wandered through the vast complex, dazed, disoriented, more dead than alive. A seemingly infinite number of corpses, left in haste, lay exposed in mass graves. The Soviets opened storerooms and found them packed with overcoats, suits, and sacks of human hair—all that remained of millions of Jews.

When the British entered the forced-labor camp of Bergen-Belsen on April 15, 1945, the bodies of thousands who had died from an epidemic of typhus (a severe disease marked by high fever and transmitted mainly by body lice) lay exposed on the camp grounds. Of the 60,000 prisoners who were found alive almost half—28,000—would die within weeks. Disease was so rampant that the camp itself had to be burned to the ground. Before they did so, however, the British, outraged by the atrocity, filmed what they'd found and broadcast it around the world.

U.S. troops who liberated other camps, including Buchenwald, Nordhausen, Ohrdruf, Landsberg, Woebblein, Flossenbürg, and Mauthausen, found equally monstrous conditions. An American journalist named Fred Friendly, who toured one of these camps, gave a chilling account of what he witnessed:

I saw the shower room where 150 prisoners at a time were disrobed and ordered in for a shower which never gushed forth from the sprinklers because the chemical was gas. When they ran out of gas, they merely sucked all of the air out of the room. I talked to the Jews who worked in the crematory, one room adjacent, where six and seven bodies at a time were burned. They gave these jobs to Jews because they all died anyhow. I saw their emaciated bodies in piles like cords of wood. I saw the living skeletons, some of whom, regardless of our medical corps' work, will die. I saw where they lived, I saw where the sick died, three and four in a bed, no toilets, no nothing. I saw the look in their eyes.

U.S. generals Dwight D. Eisenhower, Omar Bradley, and George Patton traveled to Ohrdruf to see for themselves the atrocities committed by the Nazis. What they saw sickened them. Eisenhower in particular insisted on seeing everything: he wanted to be sure that if ever there was an attempt to deny or sanitize the truth about the Nazis' barbarity, he would be able to unequivocally refute it. After his tour he said, "We are told that the American soldier does not know what he was fighting for. Now, at least he will know what he is fighting against."

More than two years before, the Allies had vowed to bring Nazi leaders to justice after the war ended. Shortly after Germany's surrender, the Allies fulfilled their promise and convened an international military tribunal, established expressly to bring to trial Nazi Party officials, military leaders, cabinet members, and heads of occupied territories.

In the fall of 1945, 22 high-ranking Nazis were indicted and tried on three types of charges: crimes against the peace, meaning the planning and waging of an illegal war; war crimes, meaning conduct violating the accepted rules of warfare, such as using prisoners for slave labor, ill treatment

of prisoners of war, the murder of prisoners of war, and theft of property and possessions; and crimes against humanity, a subset of war crimes that included charges of deportation, enslavement, murder, and extermination of civilians. Crimes against humanity also covered persecution on religious, political, or cultural grounds.

Those indicted by the international tribunal included Nazi leader Hermann Göring; Poland's governor-general, Hans Frank; *Der Stürmer* editor Julius Streicher; Foreign Minister Joachim von Ribbentrop; Ernst Kaltenbrunner, head of the Reich Central Security Office of the SS; and Wilhelm Keitel, chief of the German Armed Forces High

"Staring at the human debris on the ground awaiting burial," a soldier of the American 104th Infantry Division recalled of the day his unit liberated Nordhausen, "I asked myself, 'Is this what is meant by genocide?'"

Civilian and military leaders of the defeated Third Reich listen to testimony from the defendants' dock during the Nuremberg war-crimes trials. The landmark trials sprang from the Allies' determination to hold accountable those who had started World War II and who had conceived and implemented the Final Solution.

Command. Others who would have been indicted were already dead or missing: Adolf Hitler, Heinrich Himmler, and Joseph Goebbels had committed suicide; Czech partisans had assassinated Reinhard Heydrich in 1942. Those listed as missing included Josef Mengele and Adolf Eichmann (who was later captured by the Israeli secret service and convicted and hanged in 1962).

The first trial opened on November 20, 1945, in Nuremberg—the same city where laws against Jews had first been enacted in 1935, and where Hitler had staged his grand rallies each year. Presiding over the trial at the Palace of Justice were justices from Great Britain, France, the Soviet Union, and the United States. After all the indictments were read, the chief prosecutor for the United States, Justice Robert H. Jackson, delivered the opening statement:

> The privilege of opening the first trial in history for crimes against the peace of the world imposes a grave responsibility. The wrongs which we seek to condemn and punish have been so calculated, so malignant, and so devastating, that civilization cannot tolerate their being ignored because it cannot survive their being repeated. That four great nations, flushed with victory and stung with injury, stay the hand of vengeance and voluntarily submit their captive enemies to the judgment of the law is one of the most significant tributes that Power has ever paid to Reason.

The trial lasted 10 months, during which time countless survivors and witnesses to the crimes testified against the Nazis. More than 4,000 documents, detailing the crimes of the Third Reich from its own participants, were placed into evidence. Much of the testimony of the defendants themselves reinforced the enormity of the crimes. Still, those indicted repeatedly insisted that they had committed no crime. They were only following Hitler's orders, they said.

In the final verdicts, 10 of the defendants, including Hermann Göring, Hans Frank, Wilhelm Keitel, Ernst Kaltenbrunner, Julius Streicher, and Joachim von Ribbentrop, were sentenced to die by hanging. Others—including Rudolf Hess, Hitler's deputy *Führer,* and Albert Speer, Germany's minister of armaments and war production—were given prison sentences ranging from 10 years to life. The day before his execution, Göring committed suicide by taking a cyanide capsule. The rest were hanged in October 1946.

The end of World War II and the liberation of

inmates in the concentration and death camps brought new problems to the millions of Europeans who had been displaced, deported, or imprisoned during the war. More than a million Jews no longer had homes to which they could return: their towns and communities had been destroyed, their possessions had been seized, and their former houses were now occupied by strangers. With nowhere to go, many Holocaust survivors ended up once more staying in or near the very camps where they had been imprisoned; now, however, they had been fashioned into makeshift displaced persons (DP) compounds.

Though no longer imprisoned, those in DP camps continued to suffer from the aftereffects of brutal and inhumane treatment. Many had lingering illnesses or severe physical problems as a result of their long captivity. Most endured unimaginable mental anguish as they came to terms with what they had survived, including the annihilation of their families and friends.

After all the hardships that the DPs had endured, however, there was more to come: it seemed that even the Allied nations who had freed them were unwilling to open their shores to Jewish refugees from the war. A great number of them wished to immigrate to the United States—but it would take years for them to qualify for U.S. immigration status. Great Britain refused to allow DPs to immigrate to Palestine, which was then under its control, for fear of alienating the region's Arab inhabitants.

Less than 100,000 Jews made it to the United States by the time the last DP camp was closed, seven years after World War II had ended. Although Great Britain would not officially allow Jews into Palestine, many went there anyway. By the thousands, they managed to cross national borders and flow into the region. The British labeled this movement illegal—but the new Palestinian Jews called it *Aliya Bet,* Hebrew for "a second means of ascent to the [Promised] land."

The standoff between the British government and DPs immigrating to Palestine came to a head in July 1947, when Great Britain captured the ship *Exodus,* with 4,500 concentration camp survivors aboard, and ordered it to return to Marseilles, France. When the ship reached Marseilles, however, the Jews refused to disembark and began a hunger strike. British troops used tear gas to force them off the ship. They intended to take the survivors back to Germany and deposit them at Bergen-Belsen—where, just two years earlier, British troops had liberated victims of Nazism.

Two brothers who survived Buchenwald prepare to board a ship headed for Palestine, June 1945. Even after the world knew the enormity of what had befallen Europe's Jews, many nations remained unwilling to take in Jewish refugees. But the steady stream of Holocaust survivors who immigrated to Palestine ultimately led to the creation of Israel.

Worldwide outrage at Britain's treatment of Holocaust survivors finally ended the struggle. In November 1947, the General Assembly of the newly formed United Nations (an international peace-keeping organization that replaced the League of Nations) recommended that Palestine be divided into two regions: one for Jewish settlers, the other for Arabs. The following year, 1948, the member countries of the United Nations voted to approve the partitioning. The Jews were ecstatic at having finally gained a state of their own; Arab residents, however, were greatly displeased.

In the new country of Israel, the borders opened

wide to allow unlimited immigration. The Jews had finally found a national home. Even a new homeland has its price, though: ideological and religious differences among Arabs and Jews have brought the region continual violence and great instability, which persists to this day. Despite the ongoing troubles in the Middle East, however, the establishment of the state of Israel is one of the most significant ramifications of the Holocaust.

Still, no political or government act can diminish the horrors of the Holocaust or soften the memory of the atrocities committed. To ensure that the Holocaust will not be repeated—and to guarantee that the millions of Jews and other "undesirables" who were exterminated are never forgotten—museums and memorials around the world have sprung up in the decades since World War II. They include memorials such as Yad Vashem in Jerusalem, galleries such as the United States Holocaust Memorial Museum in Washington, D.C., and organizations such as the Simon Wiesenthal Center and Steven Spielberg's Survivors of the Shoah Visual History Foundation. (*Shoah* is a Hebrew word meaning "Desolation." Many Jewish scholars now use this term because they feel that the word *Holocaust* has lost much of its significance through overuse.) These establishments aim to educate the public, not only those who were alive during the Holocaust but the generations who have come afterward, with exhibits, preserved historical documents, and the testimonies of survivors. It is vital, these groups believe, that we never forget the searing lessons of the Holocaust.

In the 1996 TV documentary *Survivors of the Holocaust,* produced by the Survivors of the Shoah Visual History Foundation, narrator Ben Kingsley

SHALL MAKE THEM KNOWN TO YOUR CHILDR
AND TO YOUR CHILDREN'S CHILDREN.

DEUTERONOMY

HERE LIES EARTH GATHERED FROM DEATH CAMPS,
CONCENTRATION CAMPS, SITES OF MASS EXECUTION,
AND GHETTOS IN NAZI-OCCUPIED EUROPE, AND
FROM CEMETERIES OF AMERICAN SOLDIERS WHO
FOUGHT AND DIED TO DEFEAT NAZI GERMANY.

describes the powerful impact of the Holocaust on the 20th century and the importance of keeping its lessons at heart:

> As we pass into the 21st century, the world, particularly Europe, will inherit an indigestible piece of history—*Shoah*—which cannot be understood, may not be forgiven, and must not be forgotten. The only gift to the spirits of the dead and the remaining survivors is to say in all grief and in all anger, this did happen.

Lest we forget: the eternal flame at the Holocaust Memorial Museum in Washington, D.C.

Chronology

1933   *January 30:* Adolf Hitler becomes Reich Chancellor of Germany

      February 28: The Reichstag passes the Law for the Protection of the People and the State, suspending constitutional and personal rights, including freedom of speech, of the press, and of assembly

      March: The Reichstag passes the Enabling Act, giving Hitler dictatorial control over Germany; first concentration camp opens in Dachau

      April: Hitler launches an official boycott of Jewish-owned shops and businesses; laws targeting "non-Aryans" are passed

      May 10: Massive book-burning rallies take place in Berlin and other cities

1934   *August 2:* German president Paul von Hindenburg dies; Hitler names himself *Führer* by combining the chancellorship and the presidency

1935   *September 15:* The Nuremburg Race Laws are decreed, depriving German Jews of their rights of citizenship and forbidding them to marry or have sexual relations with Aryans

1936   *February:* Nazi troops occupy the Rhineland

1937   *January:* Jews are banned from many professional occupations

1938   *March:* Germany completes the *Anschluss* with Austria

      April–June: Nazis pass laws requiring Jews to register all property, wealth, and businesses

      July: Representatives of many nations meet in Evian, France, to discuss the German Jewish refugee problem

      November 9–10: Kristallnacht (the Night of Broken Glass): Nazis conduct a government-sanctioned rampage against Jewish synagogues, businesses, and homes

1939   *September:* Germany invades Poland on September 1, triggering World War II

      November: Nazis begin roundup of Polish Jews and confine them to ghettos

Chronology

1941   *June 22:* German troops invade the Soviet Union, home to more than 5 million Jews; SS *Einsatzgruppen* launch a large-scale massacre of Jews and other "undesirables"

   October–November: German and Austrian Jews are deported to Polish ghettos

1942   *January 20:* At the Wannsee conference, the Nazi plan for mass extermination of European Jews is unveiled; the full-scale operation of six extermination camps begins in Poland

1943   *April 19:* The Warsaw ghetto uprising begins; Jews hold off the Nazis for almost a month

1944   *March–July:* Between May and July, 430,000 Jews are transported to Auschwitz-Birkenau, where most are killed in gas chambers

   July 23: Soviet troops liberate the inmates of the Majdanek extermination camp

1945   *April:* American troops liberate Buchenwald and Dachau death camps; on the 30th, Adolf Hitler commits suicide in a Berlin bunker

   May: American troops liberate the Mauthausen concentration camp on the 5th; two days later Germany surrenders, ending the war in Europe

   November 22: The Nuremburg war crimes trials begin

1948   *May 14:* The Jewish state of Israel is founded

Bibliography

Bachrach, Susan D. *Tell Them We Remember: The Story of the Holocaust.* Boston: Little, Brown and Co., 1994.

Berenbaum, Michael. *The World Must Know.* New York: Little, Brown and Co., 1993.

Chippendale, Neil. *Crimes Against Humanity.* Philadelphia: Chelsea House Publishers, 2001.

Cohn-Sherbok, Dan. *Understanding the Holocaust.* London: Cassell, 1999.

Eisenberg, Azriel. *Witness to the Holocaust.* New York: Pilgrim Press, 1981.

Friedrich, Otto. *The Kingdom of Auschwitz.* New York: HarperPerennial, 1994.

Gilbert, Martin, and Rabbi Marvin Hier. 1981. *Genocide.* Produced by Arnold Schwartzman and Rabbi Marvin Hier and directed by Arnold Schwartzman. Los Angeles: The Jack & Pearl Resnick Film Division of the Simon Wiesenthal Center.

Greene, Joshua M., and Shiva Kumar, eds. *Witness: Voices from the Holocaust.* New York: The Free Press, 2000.

Justman, Stewart. *The Jewish Holocaust for Beginners.* New York: Writers and Readers Publishing, 1995.

Meltzer, Milton. *Never to Forget: The Jews of the Holocaust.* New York: HarperCollins Publishers, 1976.

Merti, Betty. *Understanding the Holocaust.* Portland, Maine: J. Weston Walch, 1995.

Neville, Peter. *The Holocaust.* New York: Cambridge University Press, 1999.

Steven Spielberg, Survivors of the Shoah Visual History Foundation, and Turner Original Productions. 1996. *Survivors of the Holocaust.* Produced by June Beallor and James Moll and directed by Allan Holzman. Atlanta: Turner Original Productions.

Wepman, Dennis. *Adolf Hitler.* Philadelphia: Chelsea House Publishers, 1985.

Further Reading

Byers, Ann. *The Holocaust Camps*. Berkeley Heights, N.J.: Enslow Publishers, 1998.

Frank, Anne. *The Diary of Anne Frank*. New York: Pocket Books, 1971.

Geier, Arnold. *Heroes of the Holocaust*. New York: Berkley Books, 1998.

Harran, Marilyn J., et al. *The Holocaust Chronicle: A History in Words and Pictures*. Chicago: Publications International, Ltd., 1999.

Strahinich, Helen. *The Holocaust: Understanding and Remembering*. Berkeley Heights, N.J.: Enslow Publishers, 1996.

Tokudome, Kinue. *Courage to Remember*. St. Paul, Minn.: Paragon House, 1999.

Wiesel, Elie. *Night*. Reprint 1969. Trans. Stella Rodway. New York: Avon Books, 1960.

WEBSITES

The History Place: World War II in Europe
http://www.historyplace.com/worldwar2/timeline/ww2time.htm

The Holocaust Chronicle (companion website to book)
http://www.holocaustchronicle.org/

The Jewish Virtual Library: The Holocaust
http://www.us-israel.org/jsource/holo.html

Last Expression: Art from Auschwitz
http://lastexpression.northwestern.edu/

Simon Wiesenthal Museum of Tolerance Online/Multimedia Learning Center
http://motlc.wiesenthal.com/

Survivors of the Holocaust (Survivors of the Shoah Visual History Foundation)
http://www.superstation.com/survivors/home_content.html

ThinkQuest Library: The Holocaust—A Tragic Legacy
http://library.thinkquest.org/12663/

United States Holocaust Memorial Museum
http://www.ushmm.org/

Yad Vashem: The Holocaust Martyrs' and Heroes' Remembrance Authority
http://www.yadvashem.org/

Index

Index

Index

Picture Credits

Cover Photos: YIVO Institute for Jewish Research/USHMM Photo Archives (front cover); Dr. Robert G. Waite/ USHMM Photo Archives (front cover); and © Hulton-Deutsch Collection/Corbis (back cover)

JUDY L. HASDAY, a native of Philadelphia, Pennsylvania, received her B.A. in communications and her Ed.M. in instructional technologies from Temple University. Ms. Hasday has written many books for young adults, including the 1999 New York Public Library award-winner *James Earl Jones*. Her *Extraordinary Women Athletes,* published in 2000, received a National Social Studies Council award.

JILL MCCAFFREY has served for four years as national chairman of the Armed Forces Emergency Services of the American Red Cross. Ms. McCaffrey also serves on the board of directors for Knollwood—the Army Distaff Hall. The former Jill Ann Faulkner, a Massachusetts native, is the wife of Barry R. McCaffrey, a member of President Bill Clinton's cabinet and director of the White House Office of National Drug Control Policy. The McCaffreys are the parents of three grown children: Sean, a major in the U.S. Army; Tara, an intensive care nurse and captain in the National Guard; and Amy, a seventh grade teacher. The McCaffreys also have two grandchildren, Michael and Jack.